Fly Fishing Women

EXPLORE ALASKA

BY CECILIA "PUDGE" KLEINKAUF

Foreword by Lyla Foggia

Photography by Michael DeYoung

Dedication

To Scott, my favorite fly fishing partner

Epicenter Press is a regional press founded in Alaska whose interests include but are not limited to the arts, history, environment, and diverse cultures and lifestyles of the Pacific Northwest and high latitudes. We seek both the traditional and innovative in publishing nonfiction books, and contemporary art and photography gift books.

Publisher: Kent Sturgis
Editor: Luanne Dowling
Cover and Book Design: Elizabeth Watson, Watson Graphics
Maps: Marge Mueller, Gray Mouse Graphics
Proofreader: Sherrill Carlson
Printer: C&C Offset Printing Co., Ltd.

Library of Congress Control Number 2003103342
ISBN 0-9724944-0-5

Booksellers: This title is available from major wholesalers. Retail discounts are available from our trade distributor, Graphic Arts Center Publishing Co., PO Box 10306, Portland, OR 97210.
Phone: 800-452-3032.

PRINTED IN CHINA

First Edition
First Printing, April 2003

10 9 8 7 6 5 4 3 2 1

To order single copies of FLY FISHING WOMEN EXPLORE ALASKA, mail $19.95 plus $5.95 for shipping (WA residents add $2.25 state sales tax) to: Epicenter Press, PO Box 82368, Kenmore, WA 98028.

Discover exciting ALASKA BOOK ADVENTURES! Visit our online Alaska bookstore and art gallery at www.EpicenterPress.com, or call our 24-hour, toll-free hotline at 800-950-6663.

Visit the author's website at www.womensflyfishing.net.

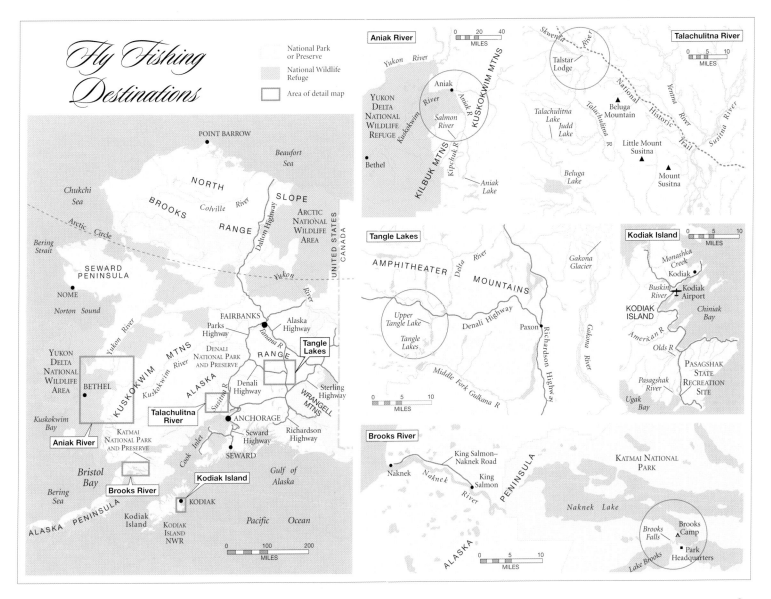

Fly Fishing Destinations

Legend:
- National Park or Preserve
- National Wildlife Refuge
- Area of detail map

Aniak River

YUKON DELTA NATIONAL WILDLIFE REFUGE
Yukon River
Kuskokwim River
Aniak
Aniak River
Salmon River
Aniak R.
Kipchuk R.
Aniak Lake
Bethel
KILBUK MTNS
KUSKOKWIM MTNS

0 20 40 MILES

Talachulitna River

Skwentna River
Talstar Lodge
National Historic Trail
Talachulitna Lake
Judd Lake
Talachulitna R.
Beluga Mountain
Little Mount Susitna
Mount Susitna
Beluga Lake
Yentna River
Susitna River

0 5 10 MILES

Tangle Lakes

AMPHITHEATER MOUNTAINS
Delta River
Gakona Glacier
Upper Tangle Lake
Tangle Lakes
Denali Highway
Paxon
Richardson Highway
Gakona River
Middle Fork Gulkana R

0 10 MILES

Kodiak Island

Monashka Creek
Kodiak
Buskin River
Kodiak Airport
KODIAK ISLAND
Chiniak Bay
American R.
Olds R.
PASAGSHAK STATE RECREATION SITE
Pasagshak River
Ugak Bay

0 5 10 MILES

Main map (Alaska):

POINT BARROW
Beaufort Sea
Chukchi Sea
NORTH SLOPE
BROOKS RANGE
Colville River
Dalton Highway
ARCTIC NATIONAL WILDLIFE AREA
ARCTIC NATIONAL WILDLIFE AREA
UNITED STATES / CANADA
Arctic Circle
Bering Strait
SEWARD PENINSULA
NOME
Norton Sound
Yukon River
Yukon River
FAIRBANKS
Parks Highway
Alaska Highway
Tanana R.
DENALI NATIONAL PARK AND PRESERVE
ALASKA RANGE
Denali Highway
Tangle Lakes
Sterling Highway
WRANGELL MTNS
Richardson Highway
YUKON DELTA NATIONAL WILDLIFE AREA
BETHEL
KUSKOKWIM MTNS
Kuskokwim River
Susitna R.
ANCHORAGE
Seward Highway
SEWARD
Cook Inlet
Kuskokwim Bay
KATMAI NATIONAL PARK AND PRESERVE
Talachulitna River
Aniak River
Bristol Bay
Bering Sea
Brooks River
ALASKA PENINSULA
Kodiak Island
KODIAK
Kodiak Island
Kodiak Island NWR
Gulf of Alaska
Pacific Ocean

0 100 200 MILES

Brooks River

Naknek
King Salmon–Naknek Road
King Salmon
Naknek River
KATMAI NATIONAL PARK
ALASKA PENINSULA
Naknek Lake
Brooks Falls
Brooks Camp
Park Headquarters
Lake Brooks

0 5 10 MILES

3

Contents

Emerald Isle and Silver Salmon 9

KODIAK ISLAND

Women pursue Alaska's acrobatic silver (coho) salmon in a variety of coastal rivers. Besides learning the tricks of identifying different types of Pacific salmon, the anglers learn to set the hook and cast heavyweight rods and big flies while fishing for these spectacular trophies.

Rainbow Revels 23

THE TALACHULITNA RIVER

This is the first Alaska river where rainbow trout were protected by catch and release. These trophy leopard trout possess amazing beauty. All novices, these women are schooled in knot tying, casting, drifting egg-imitation flies, managing split-shot while casting, hooking and landing fish, and other skills of fly fishing.

The Great Grayling Getaway 37

TANGLE LAKES

The fly fishing women master techniques of dry fly fishing for eager Arctic grayling. Rushing creeks traversing the wild, treeless hills along interior Alaska's Denali Highway offer plenty of opportunity to practice drag-free drift, line mending, safe wading, and some classic "match the hatch" techniques.

Bows and Belly Boats

FLOAT TUBING

Float tube fishing on Alaska's still waters rivals that found anywhere. Our fly fishers master the techniques of fishing from these personal watercraft, learning how to manage a tube and a fish simultaneously and how to release where there is no current to revive the fish. The wildlife-watching is a bonus!

Sockeye Stalking

THE BROOKS RIVER

No place in the world compares to Alaska's famed Brooks River. The opportunity is unparalleled to watch 1,000-pound brown bears fish for the same sockeye salmon that we two-legged anglers are pursuing. Women acquire skills for catching "un-hookable" salmon in a unique environment.

Chasing Char

THE ANIAK RIVER

Alaska's char, "fish of the rainbow," are found in the prolific Aniak River in western Alaska. A true wilderness excursion, the fly fishers enjoy the consummate fly fishing experience as they learn to read water, identify fish by both appearance and behavior, and master different casts for challenging conditions.

Foreword

FLY FISHING WOMEN EXPLORE ALASKA

I can easily imagine how proud Dame Juliana Berners would be of Pudge Kleinkauf and this book.

Five centuries ago, Dame Juliana penned the first known treatise on fishing, with step-by-step instructions on everything a novice angler would need to know, including how to build a rod, construct a hook, dye horsehairs and raid lines, and dress flies and choose patterns based on the months of the year. Indeed, the publication of this single document is regarded as the official beginning of modern sportfishing.

Following in that great tradition, Pudge is but the latest thread in an amazing dynasty of women whose words have profoundly changed the face of the sport. Among them was Sara Jane McBride, a self-educated entomologist and prize-winning fly tier who wrote the first American papers on the life cycles of insects from angler's point of view, published in leading journals in 1876.

Another, Mary Orvis Marbury, the daughter of the founder of the famous Orvis Company, compiled and authored the first definitive book on American fly patterns, which became an instant bestseller when it appeared in 1892. Significant in its impact, her effort solved an escalating crisis within the sport by creating the first standardized nomenclature for what different patterns were called at the time.

Cornelia "Fly Rod" Crosby, who was famed for her hunting and fishing skills, became one of this country's first outdoor writers and nationally-syndicated columnists in the late 1800s, as she traveled the Northeast on the Maine Central Railroad with her custom-made Charles Wheeler rod and birch bark canoe.

More recently, Joan Wulff, one of the living legends of fly fishing today, unraveled the mysteries of fly casting technique and shared her astute knowledge in several ground-breaking books on the subject.

And now, thanks to Pudge Kleinkauf, women finally have their own volume to unravel the mysteries of fly fishing Alaska, an angling paradise long regarded as a destination luring only men.

Few have spent as much time plying Alaska's awesome waters or caught as many fish as this former attorney and college professor who decided to live her passion after conquering cancer many years ago.

I have known Pudge since 1995, and long marveled at her immense love of Alaska's pristine wilderness and her dedication to the sport—particularly to introducing women to it. She is truly one of the most generous and capable anglers I've ever met, and a true role model for reel women everywhere.

Enjoy this wonderful tome as you wade through Pudge's great advice and exciting accounts of hooking Alaska's trophy salmon, rainbow, and other prized species.

And if you ever get a chance, sign up for one of Pudge's Women's Fly Fishing Alaska adventures to experience first-hand the thrill of what you're about to read. It will be a trip I promise you will never forget.

May all your reel dreams come true! See you on the water . . .

—LYLA FOGGIA,

author of *Reel Women: The World of Women Who Fish*

Emerald Isle and Silver Salmon

KODIAK ISLAND

It's too dark to see the fish," Sally whispered. "Are you sure they're there?"

"They're there, all right, but I don't know whether they're silvers," I whispered back. It was just before dawn, in a cold drizzle, and I could just barely see "v" wakes in the water. Time to be fishin'!

First light often makes coho, or silver, salmon more active, and it's usually worth getting up then to fish. But, even with our early start, we had found people at one of our favorite spots when we arrived. We could see they'd camped near the river all night in the rain, so we didn't begrudge them one of the best holes. They were equipped with head lamps to see in the pre-dawn hours and reported only spotty success so far.

We soon discovered we were early enough to take over another good section of the river. For a while the cries of "fish on" came fast and furiously. Unfortunately, most of the takers were large and very active chum salmon, not the silvers we were after. Chums are incredible. They have a bull-dog determination that makes them tiring to land. Characterized by their red-striped sides, chums are as strong but not as acrobatic as their coho cousins.

◄ *Alert for danger, a Kodiak brown bear prepares to catch fish for her cubs.*
▲ *Getting ready to fish. Dawn in Kodiak.*

Paula proved to be the only successful silver-catcher that morning. A tall, willowy woman with a lovely cast, she'd caught some sockeye salmon on another of our trips, so she was a bit more confident than the others. Nevertheless, as she fought this fish, she still felt unsure of her skills.

"I think I'm snagged up. What should I do?" she'd asked when her fly stopped drifting.

"Well, set the hook, just in case. Then try to reel, and let's see if it moves," I told her.

"I feel something. I think it's a fish," she said as her fly line quivered slightly.

It was a fish all right and, by its shine, I knew it was a coho. But instead of exploding out of the water as silvers usually do, this one just shook his head and hugged the bottom. Refusing to run, he defied Paula to pit her strength against his.

"He weighs a ton," she said.

"Well, he probably doesn't, but you're fighting both him and the current, so it seems that way," I told her. "Just keep the pressure on him." Now it was matter of whether or not she could outlast him. "Each time you feel him relax a little, try reeling. But don't be surprised if he decides to take off when you do that."

"Now go ahead and walk toward him and reel," I said. "Remember, you can't reel on a running fish. But when he's resting, walk down the bank toward him and keep reeling the whole time."

Paula got the technique immediately. "I'm supposed to reel while I walk, what next?" she asked.

"Remember 'palming' the reel from when you fished for sockeye? Well, do the same thing here. Flatten your hand and press up under the bottom of your reel to keep the spool from revolving. Then back up. That will begin to move him closer to the bank."

"He doesn't like that," Paula reported, as the fish pulled away again. "He's headed back to the middle of the river."

"Just keep control and don't let him get too far away from you," I said. "When he stops, walk toward him and reel again. Then palm and back up. Eventually he'll come in shallow enough that we can get hold of him by grabbing his tail."

After innumerable instances of "I'll pull, you pull," the fish began to approach the bank. Finally, we saw the sleek, lustrous body turn on its side in the water.

"Now!" I said. "Just palm the reel so he can't take out line, and back up the bank to pull him in. Fast. I'll hold on to you so you don't fall."

He could have turned at that point and headed for deep water, but he didn't. He was pooped. Paula didn't care that he didn't run again. All she cared was that she landed him. As she demonstrated, it's usually easier to drag the fish up the bank than use a landing net.

"Whew," she said after she succeeded, "I'm tired. Silvers really are more work than sockeye." She couldn't believe an eleven-pound fish could require so much effort on her part.

By late morning, when the action slowed, Paula's silver was our only prize. We'd caught a lot of fish, but they were chums and pink (humpy) salmon that were all well into their spawning cycle, and we put them back. Typically, everyone keeps at least one day's limit of salmon to take home, but we wanted ours to be silvers.

We were wet and somewhat discouraged. The tide had deposited heaps of smelly pink salmon carcasses on the bank, and our boots squished through them when we hiked along the river.

Just as we turned the last bend on the way to the parking area, we stopped short. Right next to the bank, a pair of chum salmon engaged in the final stages of the spawning ritual.

"Watch," Kathleen told the others who'd never seen this incredible phenomenon. "The female is swishing her tail back and forth to dig out a nest and lay her eggs. See the male hovering right next to her, waiting?"

All thoughts of fishing disappeared as the group knelt down on the bank to take in this age-old dance of procreation. Absorbed in the spectacle before them, they were almost holding their breath waiting for the first of the tiny orange globes to drop into the indentation in the gravel.

◄ *Get the fish on the beach.*
▲ *Silvers are most aggressive right at tide-water.*

"There," Sally pointed, "see the eggs emerging? They're squirting right into the nest."

"Look at the male," I told them, "he's fighting off another male eager to move into his territory. Now watch what he does."

The striped, hook-nosed buck swam in right behind the female, and, with a noticeable quiver, his whitish milt clouded the water and settled onto the glistening pile of eggs. The female quickly returned to lay another batch of eggs on top of the first. Again, they were fertilized by the waiting male. Almost exhausted, she nevertheless returned to use her powerful tail to try to cover the nest with gravel.

"Actually seeing it is way better than just hearing it explained," Henrietta said. "Such a large number of eggs must be necessary to insure that enough actually hatch. We've got to be very careful where we walk from now on, if the nests are so close to shore."

They were reluctant to leave, but finally we tiptoed away and hopped into the van to dry off, warm up, and have lunch. Then we headed for the Olds River.

KODIAK ISLAND

There are five well-known rivers and several smaller creeks accessible by car on Kodiak Island. Four of them, the Buskin, the American, the Olds, and the Pasagshak, lie south of the city of Kodiak. The fifth, Monashka Creek, reaches tidewater to the north. All have runs of salmon during the summer.

◄ *Fly casting along Kodiak's lush beaches.*
▲▲ *Kodiak Brown Bear.*
▲ *Just a small paw print.*

Because these rivers are road-accessible, they can get crowded. Local people, tourists, and residents of Kodiak's Coast Guard base all take advantage of the good fishing when the salmon are running and when the Dolly Varden char are feeding on salmon eggs.

Each river is fairly short. Because no glaciers feed Kodiak's rivers, all are crystal clear, and, unless there's been a lot of rain, they're also fairly shallow. Long, marshy salt flats that turn gold and orange in the fall characterize each river mouth, and the tidal influence affects each of these rivers for some distance up from the ocean.

The rivers are only part of Kodiak's incredible scenic beauty. Covering 3,588 square miles, Kodiak is the second largest island in the United States. First to inhabit this marine wonderland were the Alutiiq native people, who lived a subsistence lifestyle based on its riches of sea mammals, fish, and birds, and whose descendants still feature prominently in Kodiak's population. The Russian occupation in the late 1700s focused on whaling and the lucrative fur trade, but it was the development of commercial fishing opportunities in the 1800s that ultimately created modern Kodiak.

Called Alaska's Emerald Isle because of its lush vegetation, Kodiak is renowned for its large concentration of coastal brown bears. The physical environment, the relatively mild climate, and the abundance of food combine to provide the perfect location for North America's largest land mammal. Bear-watching has become a significant

draw for the area's tourists. Eco-tourism, cultural tourism, kayaking and other backcountry adventures also broaden possibilities for the excursionist on Kodiak. Besides all that, road accessible, fly-in and salt-water fishing opportunities for all five Pacific salmon species, halibut, and more make the island an angler's paradise.

▲ *Scenic Kodiak Island.*
▶ *A perfect example of a chum (dog) salmon—all stripes and big teeth.*

THE FISH

By the time we reached the Olds River everybody was ready to fish again. And here were the sea-bright silvers we were after! We could see pods of them finning in the clear water.

"You're sure they're silvers this time?" Kathleen was an experienced fly angler, having fished with me on several other Alaska trips and once in Mexico. She was too smart to wear out her arm on more chums.

"Yep, they are," I assured her. "Notice that they don't have red stripes."

The species of Pacific salmon can be differentiated from one another by certain physical characteristics. Chum salmon, averaging twelve to fourteen pounds, are identified easily by the striping that forms on the sides of both male and female fish. The male pink, or humpy, salmon is quickly recognized by the huge hump that forms on its back as it enters fresh water and heads to the spawning grounds. Pinks average about five pounds.

Sockeye, or red, salmon are the next smallest, around seven or eight pounds. (These are the fish we pursue on our Brooks River adventure.) When fresh, the sockeye can be confused with their larger cousins, the silvers, but sockeye lack the scales and the spots on their backs that characterize silvers. Later in the season, "reds" are easy to identify because of the red bodies and green heads they develop.

King or chinook salmon are the largest of the species and can weigh up to one hundred pounds, although the average is more like forty. They display large, dark spots over their entire bodies and tails and have a distinct, black line along the jaw. Where both Kings and silvers occur in the same river, smaller, sexually immature Kings are often misidentified as coho salmon and vice-versa.

Silvers tie with chums as the second largest of

the five species of Pacific salmon. Depending on the river, silvers also average in the twelve to fifteen pound range. A couple of Kodiak's rivers even produce twenty pounders. Silvers have white gums in contrast to the black-gums of Kings, and Silver's spots only occur on the top of the back and the tail. By the time we fish in the fall, the sockeye and King runs have long since passed, and we can easily distinguish between the three that are left, silvers, chums, and pink salmon.

SETTING THE HOOK

Visual identification isn't all we have to go on in differentiating among types of salmon. Each species also reacts differently to being hooked. Chums 'take' firmly and feel heavy to the angler, but they generally don't jump. Silvers, on the other hand, usually have a conniption fit the instant they feel the fly and shoot downriver like the silver bullets they are.

Reassured that they weren't fishing for chums, our group set to pursuing the silvers with gusto. A small, kelly-green fly animated the fish, and every one of the women was quickly hooking up. Not everyone was landing, however. "Ohhhhh, my fish got off," was a wail heard often amidst the whoops and hollers of other anglers.

Getting a solid hook-up in the bony mouth of a silver salmon takes some practice. Telling someone to "set the hook hard," doesn't always mean much until their fish swims off.

"Please show me again how to set the hook,"

▲ *Palming the reel to slow down the fish-run.*
▶ *Tight line on fast water.*

Sally asked after a fish she was playing came loose.

I demonstrated. "When you have a hit, tighten your fingers around the line up against the cork handle of your rod and give a short, sharp upward thrust. And don't be wimpy," I urged. "Then, once you've done that, you have to keep your rod tip high while you let the excess line slide out so that the fish can run. If you hold the line too tight, the fish will break you off or you'll get a bad line burn when he takes off."

The next time she felt something, Sally set the hook much more forcefully. As the fish ran, I advised her to "set again" to make sure the hook was firmly imbedded in its jaw.

"I think I've got him this time," she called.

And, "have him" she did. In spite of all his best efforts to dislodge the hook, Sally prevailed. The arched bend in her rod attested to his size as she landed him. "I'm not going to break my rod, am I?" she asked.

"Your rod is designed to bend like this," I replied. "But, now that you've got your fish, you must release pressure on the rod tip so it doesn't break while the fish is flopping around." I showed her how to quickly pull some fly line off her reel to create slack and avoid stressing her rod tip.

"I think I've got the hook-set thing down now," she beamed as we all admired her silvery twelve-pound beauty.

Hook-setting is only half the battle of landing salmon on a fly rod. The other half is playing and landing the fish. Everyone worked on those skills the next morning.

PLAYING THE FISH

This time the pre-dawn hours were icy cold. We'd put on long johns under our neoprene waders and donned heavy jackets, warm hats and insulated gloves. On the river, we took turns warming our hands on cups of coffee from the thermos. I was somewhat worried about Henrietta, who was from the South, but she was all bundled up and just as persistent as the rest of the group.

We'd hit the water again before the early morning "bite," but the guides in our rods were icing up in the chilly air as we cast. "Put your rod tip in the water and swish it around," I told them. "It's the easiest way to clear the guides. Otherwise, you'll just have to break out the ice with your fingers in order to cast."

Purple egg-sucking leeches and split-shot on our leaders were the morning's prescription for getting to the fish. Lorene took up a position at the head of the pool while Kathleen and Henrietta stood at mid-point and at the tailout. Sally and Paula stationed themselves in a slow run below.

Probably because of the change in atmospheric pressure, the silvers were maddeningly disinterested in our flies for a while. The pool already held a few fish from the previous evening's high water, and a few more appeared on the incoming tide. After a lot of persistence and a switch to a blue and green flash fly, things changed. Paula and Kathleen both landed fish after a long fight.

"Don't get too anxious to get him in quickly,"

I'd told them. "These fish are strong enough to just turn their heads and break your leader, if you don't take the time to play them."

Most people find it hard to let a fish run. We're always afraid we'll lose it if we do. But, having a reel with an exposed rim on the spool, like those that we use, helps keep your hand from being burned by a quickly moving fly line. It also enables you to keep a running fish under control by palming the reel instead of constantly adjusting the drag.

"Remember what you saw Paula do yesterday morning? Flatten your line hand and press up on the reel from underneath," I advised. "That slows the turns of the spool so the line doesn't pull out so fast. Don't try to completely stop your fish, just slow him down. Then, when he rests, take hold of the wind-knob again and reel fast. When he runs, let go of the knob and palm just like before. And try to keep your rod tip high to avoid giving him any slack line."

It takes a couple of fish to master all of this, but these two women did just fine. "It's easier to switch back and forth from palming to reeling than I thought," Paula remarked, flushed with victory. "Now I understand why you always say not to try to reel on a running fish. This is a lot easier. Plus, all that excitement made me forget just how cold I am."

"Well, I remember the first time I tried palming," Kathleen told the group. "I tried to slow the fish down by holding onto the wind-knob when I

▲ *Carol drifting the fly to the fish.*

should have let go and palmed the reel. The knob really rapped my knuckles. I learned my lesson the hard way."

OTHER FISHING TECHNIQUES

Another day we sat enjoying lunch in the sun-warmed grass along the bank of the American River when suddenly we saw dozens of Dolly Varden char holding in shallow riffles right in front of us. Lorene dropped her sandwich, grabbed her rod, and waded into the river. "I'm fishing," she said, "I don't care what kind they are." On her first cast she hooked a twenty-one-inch pink-spotted specimen absolutely gorged with the salmon eggs these smaller fish feed on. He was so full he regurgitated some of the shiny spheres as Lorene released him.

Lorene is an Anchorage psychologist who is an absolute fishing fanatic. She's usually the first one ready to go in the morning and the last one ready to leave in the afternoon. Up to now she'd been striking out, and was finally happy again.

As we were all getting ready to rig up to fish "Dollies," the folks on the gravel bar ahead of us called to say they were leaving their spot and that the water in front of them was full of silvers. Some were "tomatoes," as the red-sided spawning fish are referred to, but we didn't mind. We headed right over.

It often takes a good deal of frustration tolerance to fish for silvers with a fly rod. They can be active and "on" one moment, and stubbornly refuse every offering the next. Occasionally mixing and matching various techniques will work. Frequent changes in both the color and the size of the fly can also make a difference.

Using the "let the fly sink slowly and watch your line for movement" technique, Lorene was into an active ten-pound silver almost immediately.

"Hot dog," she hollered, patiently playing it in. "I'm keeping this one. It's my first silver of the day." She dragged it up on the beach, admired it, dispatched it with a blow to the back of its head, and quickly returned to the water. "I didn't feel that take at all," she reported to the others. "I just saw the line twitch and set the hook."

"Silvers often just 'mouth' the fly and then spit it out," I'd warned them earlier in the afternoon. "And they can do that without your ever feeling a thing. Watching for movement of your line is often the only way to tell they've taken the fly. And, don't worry if you set the hook and there's no fish. Better to strike too often than to miss a fish."

It worked for Lorene.

Sally, on the other hand, was successfully using the short line, extra-fast stripping retrieve that sometimes entices silvers to strike.

"Just turn your body a little so you aim down-river toward the fish and then retrieve with quick six-inch pulls of your line," I'd told her. "Silvers often like to chase the fly."

When a fleeting streak of silver alerted us that several fresh salmon had moved into the hole

▲ *Time to change flies.*

on their upriver journey, Sally was ready. A few well-placed casts resulted in two beautiful silvers on the bank for her in the next fifteen minutes.

GEAR, EQUIPMENT, AND FLIES

Fly fishing for silver and chum salmon requires quality rods and reels with a strong drag system. I recommend and use 9-ft 8-wt rods with a stiff, sturdy butt section to help you brace against fish that can weigh ten to twenty pounds. At the same time, the rod's flex must provide enough delicacy in the tip to let you feel the frequently soft bite and enjoy the incredible antics of energetic silvers.

Reels must be able to hold the # 8 line that these rods require. Their drag system must be strong enough to help fight such large fish and be able to withstand the speed with which the spools turn during a sizzling fish run. As this group learned, reels should have an exposed rim to facilitate palming. Since we often fish for silvers in salt water, good reels should also be anodized to protect against corrosion.

Generally, the only fly line needed to fish Kodiak's rivers is a weight-forward floating line. Split shot and a weighted fly sink deep enough to get to the fish most of the time. When the water is high, we occasionally use a sink-tip line. In that case, a five-foot fast-sinking tip is all that is required.

Since we wade all the rivers we fish on Kodiak Island, safe wading methods are as important a consideration as fishing techniques and equipment. We always wear collapsible wading sticks. Bungee-corded like tent poles so they can be broken down and tied to the wading belt, the sticks ride in a small belt pouch. When needed, they quickly pop into shape. Not only do they give us stability in the water, but they also enable us to measure approximate water depth before stepping forward.

A SUPER SILVER

Although Kodiak weather is typically rainy, the fall season can be gorgeous. One such day, on the drive to the Pasagshak River to intercept fish as the incoming tide swept them upriver, the scenery was breathtaking. The cottonwoods along the banks of the tiny dried-up creeks were turning orange and gold, and the dwarf maple and currant bushes glowed red beneath them in the warm sun. The hillsides were ablaze with huge patches of the burnished coppery-orange of fireweed plants gone to seed. As we turned one corner we startled two deer that bounded off into the woods and then turned to watch us with heads erect and ears outstretched.

From high vantage points along the road we could see foam-tipped breakers down along the beaches. A foggy, wet mist hung just at the horizon, penetrated here and there by shafts of late fall sun. It was gorgeous.

We didn't want to miss the tide, so we didn't stop for pictures. And, it was a good thing. We

▲▲ *Coho salmon and maribou fly.*
▲ *Male and female coho salmon.*

didn't know it then, but the fish of the trip was about to make his appearance.

Henrietta, on her first-ever fly fishing trip, (as well as her first trip to Alaska,) was casting calmly and patiently a #2 red and silver flash-fly into one of my favorite runs. All of a sudden her line stopped. By that time, she'd experienced enough hook-ups that her brain reacted by telling her arm to "set the hook, hard, now!" She realized immediately that this was no chum salmon.

With a sideways slam of his great head, this fish barreled down river like a shot out of a cannon. He hurled himself into the air a couple of times along the way to live up to the acrobatic reputation of his species.

"He's huge," Henrietta cried.

"And did you see? He's not silver; he's snow white," someone else remarked as we got a close-up glimpse of the leaping fish, "Why is that?"

I explained that the pure white color was characteristic of only the very freshest of cohos right in from the sea. Because of his size and because these newly arrived fish are always the strongest, I warned Henrietta that she was in for a real fight. She took a deep breath and settled down for the long haul.

Don't leave me," she begged.

"Not to worry," I responded. "I'm not going anywhere."

It was quite a duel, as I'd predicted, but Henrietta played this fish as though she'd been doing it all her life. She'd set the hook several

Another "super silver," dime-bright and fresh from the salt.

times, and was palming like a pro. The flex in the tip of her fly rod enabled her to experience every wriggle and gyration of this behemoth, while the butt section had the stiffness to help her fight him.

"He's head-shaking again trying to dislodge the hook," she cried. "What should I do?"

"Don't give him any slack. Keep your body facing toward him and you should be fine," I advised. "Let him run when he wants to. Just palm to keep him under control."

I didn't really need to remind her. She was careful not to succumb to the temptation to try to "horse" him in too soon. She'd learned a lot practicing on the previous day's chums, pinks, and smaller silvers. She was ready for this monster!

A cheer when up from the rest of us when Henrietta's trophy lay exhausted in the sand. "This fish hasn't spent any time at all hanging out in the estuary," I told them. He's come directly home from way out in the ocean." The sea lice along his flanks proved the point. Looking closely, we also could see he sported just a hint of the hook nose that develops so prominently on spawning males.

This fellow dwarfed our other keepers. His incredible girth and impressive length put him at nearly twenty pounds! "Wow," was about all anyone could say.

Alaska's Emerald Isle had done it again. So, it had started raining. So, we were tired and bedraggled. Nobody cared. The chance to experience a fish like this was worth it all.

Rainbow Revels

THE TALACHULITNA RIVER

In Alaska there are probably as many tales told about the Talachulitna River as any ten other rivers. Some stories are about the five species of salmon that spawn there, some are about harrowing raft trips, and some are, of course, about bear encounters. But it's the tales about the rainbow trout fishing that most vividly depict the special magic this river holds for those who've fished her. Lucky are the fly fishers who begin their learning on such a river.

THE FISHING

"He's not very big, but he's my very first trout," Barbara announced to the group. Lots of encouraging words accompanied a few quick measurements to let Barbara know that her fish was thirteen inches long. That's not a bad fish by "Lower Forty Eight" standards, but it's small for the "Tal," as this river is lovingly known. Nevertheless, it gave this group of novice fly fishers the added incentive they needed to continue casting in the pouring rain.

This was a varied group of women including a real estate agent, a housewife, an office manager, a carpenter, and a couple of health care providers.

◄ *A Tal treasure heading home.*
▲ *A nice Dolly Varden char from the Tal.*

They'd come by floatplane from Anchorage to the Tal to master this thing called fly fishing at one of our women's schools hosted by Talstar Lodge. They were already displaying that special camaraderie enjoyed by people who fish together. Rain or no rain, they were a determined bunch.

Because of their persistence, it wasn't long until Lynn hooked into a fish a couple of inches larger than Barbara's. The look of concentration on her face told the whole story, as she worked to manage the fly line hanging down from her reel and to keep the tip of her rod high at the same time. Slowly, slowly, she wound in all the line until she could play the fish from the reel without having loops and coils of line all over the place. Then she relaxed a bit and started to really enjoy the experience.

"My knuckles are white, I'm gripping the rod handle so hard," she laughed.

"So, relax," I urged her. "You're in control now.

"I knew this would be great fun," Lynn exclaimed as she worked to remove the hook from her fish after she landed it. "When I used to fish with my bait rod, I'd always watch the fly fishers.

They usually caught the most fish. They usually put them back, too. I like not having to kill fish to enjoy fishing."

Lynn, the real estate agent, was an accomplished outdoorswoman. She skied, mountain biked, and kayaked. "Fishing has always been the most relaxing of all the sports I do," she said. "Fly fishing makes that relaxation even better. It's exhilarating and challenging as well as being a great stress-reliever."

"Me too, me too," Carol suddenly cried. "I've got a fish, too. Tell me again, quick, what do I do?"

"Set the hook as we practiced and then let him run," I told her. "And, keep your rod tip up," someone else added before I had a chance to. They were learning fast!

Carol's fish treated us to a couple of spectacular jumps as it sped down the current.

"Wow, that's a much bigger fish than mine," Barbara hollered.

Carol patiently palmed her reel to slow the fish's runs and then reeled whenever he rested, just as she had learned earlier in the afternoon (with me pretending to be the fish). Closer and closer to shore she played him. Everyone gathered round to see this beauty. His flanks glistened in the crystal clear water, and the crimson lateral line, for which his species is noted, flashed and glowed as he turned this way and that. Now this was a special Tal fish.

But then, as Carol started to back up the bank, she turned her body away to look behind her. Big mistake. In a flash the fish was loose! For a breathless moment we saw him rest right at the bank, and then, realizing he was free, he high-tailed it for deeper water. No picture of this trophy, unfortunately.

"I shouldn't have turned away from him, should I?" she asked, knowing instinctively what had happened the moment he came unhooked.

"Nope," I replied. "When you turn your body you change the angle of the fly in the fish's jaw, and it frequently comes loose. But up until then, you played him just perfectly."

"I thought you only lost fish when you gave them slack," Barbara said. "Besides that and turning away from them, are there other ways you lose fish?"

"Yep," I responded, "The other most common way people lose fish is to try to 'horse them in' too quickly. Once you set the hook, you have to let the fish run or he'll break you off every time. Even a small fish can do it."

"OK, now that we know the three main ways to lose a fish, let's talk about how big this one was," Carol urged. Without measuring him, I couldn't tell them for sure, but I've seen enough Tal rainbows to know that Carol's fish was big. "Probably about nineteen or twenty inches long," I estimated. "And, by the way, I think that fish was a 'she' not a 'he.'"

"Oh yeah? How can you tell?" someone asked.

"When the fish was resting, I could see that the head and the nose were rounded. Males tend

◄ *Learning fly selection.*
▲ *Sue lets her fish run.*

to have a larger head and a more pointed nose." I explained. "You'll see."

"She certainly was gorgeous, wasn't she?" Carol reflected. "The red stripe along her side was so iridescent in the water."

Suddenly, they were all talking at once, questioning each other about measurements, about playing the fish, about how Carol knew she had a fish on, and more. These women were going to have their own tales to tell about the Tal and its famous rainbows.

As we settled ourselves along one of the favorite stretches of river we'd fish that afternoon, Ann also hooked-up. After having practiced all day, she made an absolutely perfect cast and put her fly right in the feeding line for a perfect drift. In response, the perfect fish rose to delicately sip her tiny elk-hair caddis fly.

She saw the huge nose for only a second before the lovely little side channel we were fishing absolutely erupted! Water showered into the air and down the front of her waders. Little ducks that had been swimming placidly nearby ran for cover, and Ann's fish was airborne. She hung on for dear life as it threw itself into the air.

"I was so startled I didn't remember to palm my reel," she wailed after the shock wore off. "Look how far down the river he is already."

"Just take your time," I advised. "Go ahead and start palming now, and we'll move him back toward you each time he rests. Do it gently, though, or he'll break you off," I warned, "you've only got on light tippet and this is a big fish."

As Ann calmed down, she did remember to reel only when the fish rested. With her rod tip high, she kept the fly tight in its mouth. Back and forth they went, over and over again. She palmed the reel as he sped down river and reeled each time he held still. "Golly, I'm shaking," she laughed. "I never realized how exciting catching a fish could be. This is absolutely great!" I love beginners. Their enthusiasm is so infectious.

Unlike Carol's previous experience, Ann landed this fish. It wasn't a 'him' either. Instead, it was a ravishingly beautiful female, a sleek and shimmering twenty-two-incher with a mother-of-pearl blush rouging her gill plates. It was a real coup for Ann's very first day of fly fishing.

As Ann proudly displayed her prize at the water's edge, the group had a chance to see the fish's head shape and to distinguish it from that of the males we'd been catching. But we didn't want to keep the fish out of water too long. Ann planted a quick kiss on its nose, gently and resolutely held it head first into the current until it revived, and set it free.

"Boy, you're going to be ruined forever by a fish that size for your first one," the group kidded her. Ann, a little older than the others, had told them that she'd waited all her life to take up fly fishing. Now, she was going to make the most of it. She was starting off with a bang.

Regardless of size, however, there's something

▲ *Laura's almost got him.*
▶▲ *An Alaska float plane on the Skwetna River. Our transportation to the "Tal."*
▶ *Claire Dubin's Talstar Lodge and the Tal's incredible fern forest.*

about one's first fish on a fly rod that makes it unforgettable. Barbara's thirteen-inch fish was every bit as life-changing for her as this trophy was for Ann. "Firsts" are big deals no matter what, and these women had many more to look forward to.

Being with women for these "firsts" is what makes teaching and guiding women so rewarding for me. Each time it happens, I recall my own first fish on a fly, my first fish on a fly I tied, and more. Knowing I've had a hand in introducing other women to this incredible outdoor pastime gives me a lot of satisfaction.

On the way back to the lodge we stopped at a slow glide of water that usually produces fish. Everyone was happily casting away, when Kathy's scream suddenly broke the silence.

"Ohmygosh," she gasped, "what's that?" The wide wet head and shiny ebony eyes of a large adult beaver had popped out of the water right in front of her. When we stopped to fish, no one had paid much attention to the large beaver dam situated where the river bend created a small backeddy. Now, this fellow was busy towing a small log he planned to use for damage control on his house. Our visitor looked us over, and then, with a sharp slap of his paddle-shaped tail, he let us know in no uncertain terms that we had invaded his territory.

We all found it ironic that it was Kathy, a carpenter, whom the beaver had come face to face with. Probably neither the human nor animal builder had ever been in such close proximity to their counterpart before and, for Kathy at least, her other encounters never had such directly con-frontational overtones.

"Should we leave?" Kathy asked.

"Nope," I replied, "I think he's pretty used to anglers wading along here. We just surprised him."

However, the second time he whacked the water, he was so close to her fly line that we worried he'd get hooked up. We didn't want that, so we decided it was time to head back to the lodge.

THE LODGE AND THE RIVER

No matter what time we have breakfast and no matter whether we return for lunch or take it with us to the river, we always have dinner at Talstar Lodge. Even though the group was talking at full tilt about their increasing confidence and their day's successes on the river, we were all getting tired of the persistent rain. Everyone was ready for the warming fire, the glass of wine, and the magnificent dinner that we knew awaited us.

We quickly got out of our waders and hung them inside-out to dry for the next morning. Some headed for a warm shower. Others decided that flickering, pine-scented warmth and wine were more important.

Over dinner, of course, the tales began again. We talked of where the fish had been holding, how the take had felt, how many runs or jumps each fish had made, what fly was the best to use, and

Sue shows off a nice pink salmon.

more. We toasted everyone's first fish on a fly rod as though each had been thirty inches long, and we planned our fishing expedition for the next day.

The lodge staff is used to the excitement that fly fishing engenders. Claire Dubin owns Talstar Lodge. Claire is a real Alaska woman, the kind who can haul a new generator to the lodge on a sled behind a snow machine at fifty degrees below zero. She and her first husband started the lodge. After he was killed in a plane crash, she ran the lodge herself for many years. Samantha, Claire's daughter (and one of my younger students), has grown up on the Tal. At age twelve, she caught her first king salmon on a fly rod. These folks love to see newcomers joining the fly fishing ranks. And, because of Claire's special commitment to helping women get started, and the special hospitality of the lodge, our fly fishing schools have always been held there.

Talstar Lodge is on a lower stretch of the Talachulitna River and provides both boat and wading access to the water. Its cozy log cabins are nestled among startlingly beautiful head-high ferns and brightly painted stalks of fuscia fireweed as tall as a person. It's quite a setting.

Authors, biologists, and anglers all agree that the Tal is one of the premier fly fishing streams in Southcentral Alaska. Located about sixty air miles west of Anchorage, the Tal runs from her headwaters at Beluga Mountain to the glacier-fed Skwentna River sixty-five miles away. Along the route there are rapids, canyons, and gorgeous stretches of very fishy water. Some folks fish the Tal by rafting all or part of her length; others fish only the upper stretches below Judd Lake; and some, like us, confine their activity to the lower five or six miles.

A pristine, crystal-clear waterway, the Tal is characterized by tumbling riffles, long, slow stretches with rocky bottoms, and deep, amber-colored pools near the mouth, where the salmon rest before starting their upstream spawning journey. Unless the water is high from spring runoff or heavy rains, long gravel bars covered with scrub willow bushes are good places to fish and camp. Huge cottonwood, birch, and spruce trees climb the hillsides along the banks with the overhanging willows providing shaded hideouts for migratory salmon and hungry trout. No matter which stretch of water people fish, there always will be tales of the beauty of the Tal as well as tales of her fish.

THE FISH

The excellent rainbow trout fishing in the Tal results in part from its extensive runs of Pacific salmon. Starting in June and ending in early September, all five species of Pacific salmon enter the Tal. Kings (chinook) salmon arrive first. By early July, the red (sockeye) and chum (dog) salmon typically join them. And, in even-numbered years, so do large numbers of pink salmon. The prized silver (coho) salmon appear on the

▲▲ *Measuring a trophy.*
▲ *A male pink salmon. Also known as a "humpy."*

scene near the end of July and continue through the month of August.

Spawning king salmon are always an indicator of good trout fishing, and one particular day during this school was no exception. Huge, dark, thirty-pound males jockeyed for position to fertilize the eggs a female was laying in a depression she'd made with her wide tail in the gravel. Some of these tiny red-orange globes had escaped and were bouncing down the river just below the nest. Other fish were gobbling them up as fast as they could.

The river's rainbows, Dolly Varden char, and Arctic grayling know to fall in behind these nests, or redds, to get an easy meal. Rainbows are often seen swimming up and bumping the female salmon with their noses as if to urge her to hurry up and get on with it because they're hungry.

We quickly switched from the caddis flies and nymphs we'd been using to a small imitation of those very eggs. Many fly anglers disparage egg-flies, but there is no question about their effectiveness. When the color and size of the imitation makes it a good match for the original, the trout, char, and grayling vie with each other to see who gets it first.

To our surprise, it was a lovely arctic grayling with its sail-like dorsal fin that Candy first hooked in that stretch of water. "I've never caught a grayling before," she announced as the others gathered around to marvel at this beauty. "Apparently they find salmon eggs as juicy a morsel as the trout."

▲▲ *Bobbi's first fish on a fly—a perfect silver salmon.*
▲ *A leopard rainbow on a dry fly.*

"They sure do," I replied. "But usually we just don't see many grayling in this part of the river until later in the season."

Several rainbows quickly followed the grayling's example in this productive stretch of water. "Boy, the fish really grab at this egg fly," Kathy observed. "These are hard hits. They must be afraid it will float right on by if they don't take it quickly."

"Look carefully here near the bank and watch how the real eggs move along at the same speed as the current," I told them. "The fish move from spot to spot just picking them up."

"Oh, look at this fish," Carol called to us from down river. She was knee-deep in the water carefully dislodging the hook from the lip of a chunky, broad shouldered fish. "His cheeks are absolutely crimson and so is the line along his sides," she added.

"He looks different somehow," Lynn commented. "Why is that?"

This fish, just like the one Carol had lost, was an example of the special strain of rainbows known as leopards that make the Tal such an incredible river. Unlike the 'regular' rainbows that inhabit this river, leopards usually display coloration more caramel than silver and have larger spots. Males generally have even larger heads than their silvery cousins as well as wider shoulders. Leopards also tend to sport a dazzling blood-red coloration along their lateral line and on their gill plates. Even though all the rainbows on the Tal are wild fish, catching one of the big leopards is really the stuff of fishing tales.

Rainbow fishing on the Tal nearly came to a screeching halt in the late 1960s and early 1970s as word of its riches began to spread. Suddenly, people who'd fished the river for years began noticing an alarming decrease in the number of large rainbows. More and more were being killed for trophies.

Finally, a small group of doggedly persistent fly anglers decided to do something about it before it was too late. Their repeated documentation of the decline of rainbow stocks resulted in a 1977 decision by the Board of Fish to declare the Tal a catch-and-release river for rainbow trout. It took a few years, but gradually the stocks rebounded. This success story became the basis for catch-and-release policies on many of Alaska's other rivers. While we may never again see the numbers of thirty-inch fish that made the Tal famous, incredible rainbows still populate this remarkable river.

FLIES AND KNOTS

Once the salmon are in the river and spawning, their eggs and later their flesh become the food sources that enable the trout to grow in length, size, and girth. Even if one salmon run is poor, there are four others to sustain the rainbows.

In the spring and early summer, Tal river rainbows thrive on leeches and sculpin, as well as

▲ *Here, try this fly.*
▲▲ *Black leech-flies are proven trout-catchers.*

the caddis, mayflies, and stoneflies that populate the river. Imitations of those creatures become the flies of choice. Once the salmon are spawning, however, we switch to flies that imitate the rotting salmon flesh and the salmon eggs that serve as the trouts' main course. As Ann's spectacular fish attests, rainbows may, at times, take a well-presented dry fly when eggs are present, but that is the exception rather than the norm.

Salmon eggs differ in both color and size. At any given time, Tal rainbows have the eggs of at least three different salmon to choose from. But the eggs of a thirty-pound king salmon are considerably larger than those from the five-pound pink salmon. The king eggs are also brighter initially. The longer eggs are in the water, the more they bleach out, however. So it's often hard to decide just which of the veritable smorgasbord of eggs the fish actually are eating on any particular day.

We tie our imitations on small, short-shanked hooks, sizes 6-10, in colors from bright salmon pink to pale butterscotch. It's frequently necessary to try out eggs in different sizes or different colors until we find just which one works.

Besides copying the salmon eggs, we also imitate the flesh of the rotting salmon. The later in the summer it is, the more dead and decaying salmon carcasses the river contains. Disgusting as it may sound, this protein-rich food source is prized by the gorging rainbows.

The best flesh imitation is the size 6 or

8 white fly made with strips of bunny fur. At times we add a chenille egg to the head of that bunny to create a fly known as the egg-sucking bunny. It doesn't matter that no one has ever seen a bunny eating an egg, both the plain and the egg-headed version have proven irresistible to lots and lots of hungry trout.

That fly is exactly what resulted in one of Candy's best hook-ups. She'd been fishing in a good stretch of water and had hooked and landed several fish on small egg flies.

"I'm getting tired of fishing with egg flies," she said after going fifteen minutes without a fish. Because we'd had a lesson that morning on some of the different flies that attract rainbows, I offered her my fly box and told her to go ahead and choose something else.

"I'll take one of these big egg-sucking bunnies," she decided. "Mostly because I think the name is so funny. A funny bunny."

Three casts later, she learned that the fish didn't think the fly was funny at all. They thought it was dynamite. That fly was heading out, stuck hard in the jaw of a big, strong rainbow. The bend in Candy's five-weight rod indicated the possibility of another one of the twenty-inch plus fish the Tal is famous for.

"This is a bigger fish than my others," she reported. "I'll bet he was just waiting for a larger morsel." The aggressiveness of his strike, and the speed of his run were proving her correct.

Unfortunately, though, Candy got worried

▲ ▲ *A nice pair of bright silvers.*
▲ *A bow to be proud of.*
▶ ▲ *Let's try that cast again.*
▶ *Practicing catch and release.*

about the velocity with which the fish was traveling. As a result, she palmed her reel just a little too hard and her knot broke from the pressure.

"Oh, no," she cried. "I must not have been careful enough the last time I tied on a tippet. Not only is my fish gone, but now I'll have to get out of the water and tie a new tippet on my leader."

Our knot-tying lesson the previous night had resulted in the group mastering the knots required to construct their own leaders and tippets and tie on their own flies. They'd practiced and practiced until I declared their nail, blood, and improved clinch knots perfect. Now their efforts were put to the real test, and Candy's blood knot had failed her.

Candy had been spin-angler before taking up fly fishing. She was not used to the careful patience it usually takes to land a large fish on small diameter leader on a fly rod. "Let's get to work on a new leader," I told her. "I'll help you if you get stuck."

"Remember, after you make the "x," you have to make five wraps and poke the line through the hole going all in the same direction," I reminded her, as she got to work on her blood knot with eight-pound and six-pound test monofilament line. This lesson took place as we sat on a huge cottonwood log that had been deposited on the bank by the spring floods. "Then after you change hands, the second set of wraps and poke through the hole have to go in the opposite direction."

"I remember," she replied. "Guess I was in too

big a hurry to get back on the water last time. I'll certainly be more careful from now on. I never want to lose a great fish like that again because my knot broke."

I couldn't help but wish that she hadn't had to learn such an important lesson in such a hard way.

"Check your knot when you get done," I reminded her. "If the short pieces of monofilament are coming out the top of the knot instead of out the sides, your knot won't hold."

"I forgot to do that last time," she replied. "Maybe that's what my problem was. But it's perfect this time. I'm ready to go."

THE GEAR AND THE TECHNIQUES

Rainbow fishing on the Tal requires a 9-foot, 5- or 6-weight rod, a reel with a good drag system, a matching floating line, and, typically a small split shot or two on the leader. Unless the water is high, we seldom revert to using sink tip lines. It's the tippet and the fly that make the difference between success and failure.

Leaders that are seven or eight feet long are usually adequate to fish the Tal's rainbows. The leader must taper to a six-pound (3X) tippet if the water is low and clear, however, so the wary rainbows don't spot it. This type of water can also dictate another foot or two of leader to keep an egg fly drifting naturally.

Drag-free drift is the most important requirement of fishing with egg imitations. Many fly fishers associate that concept only with top-water

flies, but it's just as important with flies fished under the surface. If the egg or flesh imitation doesn't drift naturally, the fish ignore it.

"I think I 'get' this drag free drift thing," Ann decided. "The natural eggs swept out of the redds just bounce and roll along the current at the bottom of the river. Our imitations have to do the same thing or they don't look right to the fish. It's sort of like when we worked to get our dry fly floating without any 'v' wake."

"Right you are," I said. "These eggs are the fish's major food source, and it's not easy to fool them. And, believe it or not, your fly can also have the old 'v' wake underwater."

"So I still have to mend my line after I cast and keep the line from coming tight just like we did with the caddis." Lynn observed. They caught on quickly.

Often split-shot are necessary to reach the bottom and stay there with the tiny ball of pinkish fuzz that represents the salmon egg. Fly anglers hate split shot because it's hard to cast and often affects the drift of the fly. It's a necessary evil, however, so we must master both casting and fishing with it.

Casting split shot with the basic overhead cast requires slowing the cast and opening the loop just slightly. Otherwise, the split shot will hit the rod, the angler, or both. The technique of "waiting for the bounce" of the line (produced by the weight of the shot as the fly turns over) is a time-honored tip in Alaska for dealing with split shot.

▲ ▲ *Stripping the line as the fly moves along.*
▲ *The rods are rigged and ready to go.*

We do as little overhead casting with split shot as possible, however, preferring to substitute a cast we in Alaska call the Russian River Flip. That's a cast that simply "flips" the fly and the split shot into the water with either a side arm or a rollover motion. Once in the water, the angler drifts the egg with the technique used for fishing nymphs.

"OK, so how come my fly and split shot landed on the other side of the river?" Lynn wondered as she tried to cast to some rainbows holding behind a pod of spawning salmon.

"Your technique is fine," I told her, "just don't 'flip' with so much force. The split shot really pulls a lot of line out if you're too enthusiastic with this cast."

A few practice casts later, her fly was in the water where she wanted it. She then reverted to essentially the same drift technique we'd been using for fishing nymphs with a short line, an upstream cast, and a rod held perpendicular to the water to achieve a line that hangs straight down when the egg fly bounces in front of her. Just as it drifted on past her, an eager and feisty rainbow picked it up.

"It's show time," she cried as her fish made a twisting, turning leap into the air. With what seemed like no effort at all, he was quickly holding tight about twenty-five feet down river from her.

"I can see your fish here right in front of me," Barbara called out. "One of the salmon keeps trying to run him off. Better get him in fast or you're liable to loose him."

Lynn got down to business and soon had a nice bend in her rod as she landed the fish. "Another beauty," she whispered in awe and then sent him home to be there for another day.

No matter the time of year, the fly, the angler's fishing experience, or the particular techniques used, to fish the Tal is to be spoiled forever. She was the first river I ever fly fished in Alaska, and I've been her faithful servant ever since. I feel privileged to introduce others to the pleasures of fly fishing in such a special place.

Although no two years are ever quite the same, her dusky pools and wadeable riffles call me back again and again. At times she changes course, and at times low water reveals her secret depths. At other times she humbles us with water so high and cloudy that it's impossible to figure out where she's hiding her treasures. Nevertheless, I always go back.

Each visit brings unique encounters with the red fox kits watching us from the willows or with the eagles waiting in the trees for our fish remains. Maybe we'll see the black bear that patrols the far bank at the river's mouth or the family of river otters sliding effortlessly off muddy banks and slick rocks. These creatures make us feel a part of the community and enliven every fishing excursion. And, of course, besides these other residents, we always encounter those incredible fish. The tales never end.

▲ *A great class photo.*

The Great Grayling Getaway

TANGLE LAKES

I could play with these fish all day," Teresa remarked, as yet another grayling delicately took her #12 elk hair caddis. "They're so willing. Besides, this is a lot more fun than selling insurance."

Teresa and the other women in the group had put up the tents and rigged the fly rods during a letup in the rain and were now fishing in a light drizzle. The grayling in the Tangle River along Alaska's Denali Highway were eager to cooperate. Nevertheless, they were quite picky, and our group got few hook-ups at the beginning. Some of the women couldn't see the rises, some couldn't put their fly square in the fish's feeding lane, and some were having trouble with what is known as the drag-free drift. Sitting around the picnic table our group had discussed accuracy, mending line, and fly-before-leader delivery, but on-the-water practice was required before the catching would begin. Thank goodness the fish were so patient.

SPOTTING THE RISE AND FISHING TO IT

The successful grayling fly fisher must first learn to spot the rise forms. That really isn't too difficult as Arctic grayling are voracious, albeit delicate, feeders.

◄ *The fish are out there, just waiting for my fly.*
▲ *I'll master this clinch-knot yet.*

"Just focus on the water in front of you," I told them. "Pick out a small section of river and watch it as intently as you can. Look for little dimples or bubbles on a surface that just previously was undisturbed. And once you see something, keep your eye fixed on that spot to see if it happens again."

I'd just finished that instruction when Annette hollered, "There's a rise. I can see it. And, there it is again!"

"Okay," I said, "now describe it for the others."

"Well," she began, "it was just a little swirl on the surface. I only noticed it because I was really concentrating," she added.

"Where was it?" someone asked.

"Right there," Annette pointed with her rod tip. "Oh, there it is again."

"I see it now," Karen said.

"Me too," added someone else.

"Now watch a different piece of water and see if you can see something similar," I suggested to the group. "That's the way to locate the fish."

Dimples, swirls, and blips marked the places where the grayling found their sustenance and identified the feeding lanes for the anglers.

Soon everyone could spot the rises, and they were ready to try to put their flies on the water and drift them to those rises. This is more easily said than done, however. Because of their relatively small size, grayling occupy narrow feeding lanes and generally will not move laterally to take a fly. They line up, largest first, along particularly good food-producing currents and stay there. The fly fisher must place her fly directly along that path.

"Your eye has to develop a sense of the right distance for the cast, so your fly will land where you want it to," I told them all. "Start by measuring out about how much line you think you'll need to get to the spot you want. Then see if your fly ends up where you aimed or if it lands too short or too long."

"Well, my fly landed way on the other side of the spot I was casting to," Teresa said.

"Remember to add the length of your leader into your calculation," I suggested. "Shorten up your line a little and try again. Point your thumb at the spot you're casting to, and don't look away while you're casting."

"Boy, I have to locate the fly the instant it hits the water and then never take my eye off it, or I lose it in the little waves," Fran remarked as she cast.

And she was right. Riffles, currents, and the glare of light on water complicated her ability to focus on the tiny dry fly as it drifted along.

"Well, the farther away from me the fly lands, the harder time I have locating it," Teresa responded.

Each had identified part of the difficulty. "Try not to make too long a cast so you can easily spot the fly just as it hits the water," I told them. "Then keep your eye on it as it drifts along. Once you get the hang of it, you can lengthen your cast."

Karen had selected a spot where the water dropped off a small rock ledge and then continued down a beautiful slow run. Fish rises dimpled the water everywhere.

"I can sure see why accuracy is essential," she commented as I waded down to see how she was doing. "If my fly is even a couple of inches out of the zone, the fish won't move to get it. It really is important to be 'right on.'"

"Well, at least the fish don't move away if I miss the spot," Dee chimed in. "They just keep rising to show me where they are while I try to get my fly in the correct place." Then suddenly, her rod tip danced with what turned out to be a lovely grayling with burnished-gold gill plates and fuscia-tipped fins. "I'm glad he waited for me to get it right," she beamed as she reeled it in.

ARCTIC GRAYLING

Characterized by an elegant, sail-like dorsal fin, Arctic grayling are gorgeous creatures. They shimmer brightly with iridescent aqua colors that absolutely glow in the water. That color disappears almost immediately when the fish are taken from the water, however, and photographs simply don't do them justice.

Anglers who have never fished in Alaska rarely

◄ *Easy rigging, rod, reel, and line in a great carrying case*
▲ *It's the group that makes the trip so special.*

know this delicate beauty. Once experienced, however, grayling quickly become a favorite for dry fly fishing.

Grayling are members of the whitefish family. They are the slowest growing of Alaska's sport fish in spite of their reputation for being the most consistently voracious feeders of any fresh water fish. It does often seem that they'll take anything we throw at them. Still, they're not big fish.

Studies show that a twelve-inch fish is probably already five to six years old, while a nineteen-inch fish can be ten years old or more. A fish over eighteen inches in length is considered a trophy. In Tangle Lakes, the fish average ten to fifteen inches in length. Their size can probably be attributed to their harsh environment and their failure to feed in winter.

Just because grayling are small fish doesn't mean they can't put a real bend in a 5-weight rod. Their eagerness to take a properly presented fly and their plucky spirit when hooked make them a favored sport fish of Alaskans and visitors alike.

THE DRAG-FREE DRIFT

"Well, they must not like what I'm serving," Annette said as she started to change flies. "My fly is right in the feeding lane and they still won't take it."

"Cast again and let's watch your fly," I suggested.

Grayling are wonderful teachers of proper presentation. They generally ignore a dragging fly or one where line or leader are visible to them. The fly fisher must be constantly on the alert for that moment when the line and leader become tight, holding the fly back and keeping it from floating freely. In addition, differing currents between the angler and the fly frequently cause the leader or line to float down ahead of or perpendicular to the fly. Both occurrences make fish wary. Sure enough, Annette's fly was dragging. The tell-tale "v" wake had formed behind her elk-hair caddis.

"See the 'v' in the water behind your fly?" I asked. "That's one reason the fish won't take it. And notice how your leader is floating right beside the fly. The fish can see it. They know the real bug doesn't drag and it isn't attached to monofilament. So, let's work on your line-mending."

The technique called "mending" usually cures both the problem of the fish seeing the leader and also the problem of drag. Mending involves gently rolling the rod tip upstream of the fly in order to position the leader and the line so they float behind the fly. Then, you point the rod tip at the drifting fly to keep the line from tightening and holding back the fly. The result is that the fish sees only a naturally drifting fly.

More than one fly fisher has cast and cast before perfecting a drag-free drift. And more than one of our group was frustrated by pulling a wispy, weightless dry fly completely out of the water while learning to mend line and leader. It takes practice and patience to master this

◄ *The fly fishers' nemesis, a fly in the bushes.*
▲ *An exquisite Arctic grayling.*

important skill. Annette had ample measures of both. She was determined to get this, and she did.

Fran also had practiced and practiced the skill of mending to get her leader behind her fly and now was enjoying the fruits of her efforts.

"There he is," she cried as a grayling rose up over her fly. He gracefully inhaled it and dove back into the water. "But I didn't get him," she lamented when her line went slack. "Now what did I do wrong?"

Annette, a teacher, and Fran, a nurse, were neighbors and friends. They had come on the trip to build their skills and their confidence so that they could go fish together, and they were doing just fine. Constantly comparing notes and helping each other, they'd both been having lots of "hits and misses." There was one more skill to learn.

"You struck a little too quickly," I replied. "Grayling have a tendency to take the fly as they're diving and not as they're rising. Wait just a second or two longer before setting the hook."

With first-rate Polaroid sunglasses and focused concentration they began to see the grayling come from under the surface of the water and swirl toward their fly. They were quick to notice the fish's tendency to take the fly as it returned to the river bottom.

"Okay, I've got him this time," Fran said, three casts later, hooking and landing a sixteen-inch fish, the largest of the day.

As the group learned the essential skills for dry-fly fishing, we wandered farther afield. Next

▲ *A perfect cast in a perfect setting.*

morning, we hiked down and fished the lower Tangle River. It rushes and tumbles along a rocky, meandering course interspersed by small brushy islands. This morning, one such place proved to the liking of a great horned owl. He sat stoically in an alder, chewed to a stump by a browsing moose, and watched us intently. It was amazing how close we got to him before he lazily flew away.

The slightly rusty colored water in the Tangle River, in riffles and pools shadowed by birch, alder, and willow, makes for perfect grayling habitat. Just as our group spread out along one great stretch of water, a large, tan, caddis fly began to hatch. Soon the air was filled with bugs, and fish rose to take them on every square inch of water.

"This is the test to see what we learned yesterday," Karen commented. "I can see fish rises in so many different feeding lanes it's actually hard to pick just one to cast to."

"And be accurate, and get a drag-free drift," Dee reminded her.

Dee had been fly fishing for salmon, and decided she wanted actually to see the fish take the fly for a change. Knowing that grayling fishing provides the best opportunity to do that, she'd come on this trip to master "that dry fly thing."

"I love the light rods and the tiny flies," she reported. "I feel like this is the next important step in my evolution as a fly fisher."

Carefully she selected her feeding lane, screwed up her forehead in concentration and placed her fly exactly where she wanted it. It hadn't gone far when a beautifully tapered head followed by a dorsal fin in full sail rose to take it. "Well, now I think I finally understand what a 'hatch' is," Dee mused as we looked down the line through a haze of fluttering caddis wings to see every single rod playing a fish.

THE GRAYLING HIGHWAY

Since Arctic grayling thrive only the purest, coldest streams, they find the perfect environment along Alaska's Denali Highway. The place where my son caught his first fish on a fly rod, the Tangle River continues to provide an outstanding opportunity for those beginning their journey as a dry-fly fisher. Besides being a premier dry-fly fishery for grayling, however, this region of the highway is also a scenic delight. The area is a six-hour drive north from Anchorage on a hummocky, paved road that's turned to corduroy by winter frost heaves. There is more to savor here than exquisite fish.

Just west of the tiny hamlet of Paxson, the first pullout along the Denali Highway provides a stunning introduction to the area. On a clear day, its views of the Gakona Glacier and Icefall Peak rise above an unbelievable sweep of lakes and mountains.

The entire 130-mile length of the highway reveals similar panoramas. At about milepost 55, travelers cross the McClaren Summit, the highest road in Alaska before the trans-Alaska pipeline was built. The view from the top extends across tiered rock and lake formations that descend to

▲ *Heading down the Denali.*

the mighty McClaren River, then rises again to the distant glaciers, whose retreat carved out this extraordinary vista.

The glaciers, mountain ranges, high plateau lakes, and meandering creeks and rivers (all filled with grayling) make the area a feast for the eye and the soul for all who venture here. Cut banks, dotted by the nests of mud swallows, and hills with constantly shifting shadow patterns decorate the roadway. Only the speed limit of thirty miles per hour prevents people from going off the road as they gawk at the splendor.

At certain times another spectacle unfolds as well. Early July, when we make our annual safari, is the prime time for wildflowers. By then, the late spring runoff is past and the creeks and rivers have cleared. Wildflowers of every color and size lie hidden among the willows or sprout along the creek banks. Some are such wee things they remain virtually invisible until we're actually sitting amidst them.

Along roadside and hillside, lavender or butter-yellow blossoms wave in the breeze. Yellow and purple arnica, monkshood, wild geranium, star flowers, and tiny violets, as well as blueberry and cloudberry blossoms and many others thrive in this incomparable ecosystem. A wildflower book is always in my fishing vest.

NYMPHING

Although we go to Tangle Lakes primarily for the dry fly fishing, nymphing techniques are also

part of the curriculum. Another group of women was particularly glad of that during an unusually cold trip when the dry-fly fishing wasn't up to par.

"The fish are still feeding," I told them. "They're just doing it under the surface. So, let's copy the immature stage of the bugs and get down there with a nymph instead of a dry fly."

Learning to feel the fish take the fly when you can't see it happen is one of the essential skills of nymph fishing. Some use a strike indicator similar to a bobber on the leader to signal that a fish has taken the fly. But that really isn't necessary with grayling. Reliance on a strike indicator actually can hinder the development of two essential fly fishing skills—developing a "feel" for the take and learning to watch for subtle movement of the line.

Nymphing is most successful when you use a relatively short amount of line (typically nine or ten feet long) with five or six feet of leader. You cast slightly upstream to give the fly time to sink, and then bounce the fly along the bottom. That's where the real nymphs are, and that is where the fish expect to see them.

"Sometimes I feel the fish hit, but, even if I don't, I can see the line twitch when I've got a fish," said Jodi. "I've always passed up faster water because my dry fly went by the fish too quickly. I won't do that any more."

"Often the largest fish are caught deep in fast water if you can get down to them," I told her. "The water at the bottom is never as fast as the

◄ *Denali—North America's highest peak.*
▲ *Ideal grayling water.*

water at the top, and there's a lot of fish-food down there."

The hook-ups came fast and furiously for them all, once they learned to rely on feel and line movement. This group certainly didn't need strike indicators to tell them a grayling had taken their nymphs.

Maureen hollered that she'd wanted to learn to do this as she landed her fifth grayling from the depths of a great run of foam-tipped riffles below a rock. A #10 gold-ribbed hare's ear with a small split-shot on her leader had the fish doing her bidding.

"Maureen, don't move," Jodi said softly from across the river as Maureen prepared to cast into the riffles once more. Fearing the appearance of a bear, Maureen froze.

"What is it? What is it?" she whispered. "Is it a bear?"

"Something much better," Jodi replied. "It's a beautiful red fox right behind you."

Sure enough, everyone but Maureen could see the black nose, the bushy, white-tipped tail, and the glossy, red-orange coat of a large fox that had emerged from the bushes right behind her. He proceeded to plop down on his haunches to watch her fish and licked his chops noisily, perhaps in anticipation of a fat grayling for lunch.

Maureen slowly turned her head so she could see him. When she quietly said hello, he cocked his head first on one side and then the other listening to her. We all had the feeling that he had conversed with anglers in this spot before.

He seemed to understand as Maureen told him that she didn't have a fish for him because she was putting them all back. Following that declaration, he lazily rose and ambled along the bank awhile before disappearing into the bushes.

That evening, in the long summer sunlight, when a few mayflies were hatching, Glenda was the first to remember that a pheasant-tail nymph imitated the immature stage of a mayfly. So, that's what she tied on to fish with. It was a good choice.

Glenda has admirable patience, an important characteristic for a fly angler. A longtime Alaskan, she took up fly fishing after finding that fishing with a spinning rig just wasn't interesting enough for her. She and her husband, owners of a printing business, have a cabin on one of Southcentral Alaska's best-known lakes. She easily transferred her fly fishing skills to that environment and particularly likes the fact that her husband generally rows the boat so that she can cast. "Not many people have their own private guide all the time," she says of him.

"This fish really hit that nymph," Glenda reported to the others, as she showed off the huge colorful dorsal fin before releasing her seventeen-inch fish. "You all had better switch flies."

And switch they did. Elaine and Janet, two friends from Oregon traveling around Alaska, had come on the trip to have a chance to fish for a species they'd never seen before. They'd watched Glenda carefully as she'd played her large fish and wanted to do the same. They'd located a beautiful

▲ *A grayling that took a nymph.*

run to fish, but it was fronted by heavy brush that prevented them from making a back cast. Unable to cross the river and fish from the other side because of a very fast current, they effectively used their steeple and roll casts to present their nymphs to the waiting fish.

"I'll certainly have this fly in my box from now on," Elaine announced as her line came tight on an aggressive fifteen-inch fish. "And, after this trip, I also know how to fish it."

"Me, too," Janet chimed in. "But darn it, I'm in the trees again. I think I still need help with my steeple cast."

"Remember, in the steeple cast, there's no back cast," I reminded her. "Send your rod tip up to 12:00 o'clock instead of back to 1:00. Then slope down to 11:00 o'clock and stop there before letting your line fall on the water."

"Better, much better," she critiqued herself as she changed from a back cast to the upward thrust of the steeple. "I'll get 'em now," she murmured.

EQUIPMENT, FLIES, AND GEAR

Although the pheasant tail-nymph is incredible effective at times, the "never leave home without it" fly for grayling in Alaska is definitely a #12 elk-hair caddis. But the same size humpies with red, yellow, or gray bellies, royal wulffs, irresistibles, adams, and a stimulator-type fly called the Tangle Lakes Teaser are successful too. In Alaska, we don't have to use the much smaller size flies that are required in "Lower 48" fishing. Our fish aren't as picky. Nevertheless, flotant becomes our most important accessory.

Many of our flies are tied with white wings or a white calf-tail post for easier visibility in the riffles. These noticeable flies were initially Maureen's first choice, because she had forgotten her Polaroid glasses. I dug around in my van and finally located a spare pair for her. Then, she, too, could fish successfully with even the hard-to-see flies.

There's really only one nymph needed to fish for grayling, as the group found out: a #10 or 12 gold-ribbed hares ear. Zug bugs (a fly that only vaguely resembles a stonefly nymph), also in a #10, are always in our nymph box, as are those pheasant tails that Glenda preferred, and the soft hackle fly with an orange, yellow, or olive body.

A 9-foot, 4- or 5-weight fly rod is perfect for grayling. The more delicate the tip, the more fun grayling fishing is. I caution against using the newly popular one-weight rods, however, because landing a fish takes longer on such rods. Grayling fight fiercely for their size and can exhaust themselves quickly. Anglers may learn to their dismay that even with the best catch and release techniques, this beautiful specimen of the north cannot be revived when played too long on too light tackle.

At times, it seems that the grayling are so plentiful they couldn't possibly be a vulnerable species, and people get careless. If only they could see grayling spawn, I think they'd move heaven and earth to protect them.

▲▲ *I love grayling fishing.*
▲ *Beautiful water, beautiful fish.*

Grayling pair up and hide away in tiny, private spots to complete this ageless ritual. Unlike other fish species, the female doesn't dig a nest for her eggs when she arrives at the spawning beds in the spring. Instead, she simply drops 4,000 to 5,000 tiny, sticky eggs, which adhere to the gravel. As the male swims close beside her to spread his sperm over the newly laid eggs, he ardently drapes that beautiful dorsal fin protectively over her body in a incredible display of pairing. To me, that simple manifestation of tenderness is even more unique than the sticky-egg, no-nest phenomenon that many write about.

The eggs can come un-stuck easily if spring run off or heavy rains increase the water flow. The tiny fry, born just two to three weeks after the eggs are dropped, also are at risk from higher water.

Although there's nothing we can do about water flow, we can help preserve this special fish by fishing with single, barbless hooks, practicing catch and release, and limiting our kill rather than killing our limit.

CONSTANTLY FEEDING

Truly the Arctic grayling is a unique and delicate fish worth safeguarding. We revere it both for its beauty and its willingness to take our flies. Biologists account for a grayling's appetite by describing its lifestyle.

Grayling spend the winter in deep pools under the ice but feed very little during that time. They survive there in oxygen levels lower than any other salmonid. Because grayling spawn in the spring, they must feed ravenously all summer to develop the eggs and sperm for the following year's spawning before winter arrives. No wonder they're eating all the time.

While grayling will eat almost any invertebrates, their preferred diet is aquatic and terrestrial insects, in all stages of development. Grayling that inhabit salmon spawning streams also put salmon eggs high on their list of favorites. In a number of Alaskan streams large grayling have even been found with small lemmings in their stomach.

Typically we fish for grayling with dry flies and nymph imitations of caddis flies, but mayflies and stoneflies also occur along Alaska's rivers. Early one morning in late-June, one of the women who was sharing my tent whispered me awake. "Pudge, Pudge," Tanya said, "wake up." Fearing a large, brown visitor, I was quickly alert. "Look. There, on the tent-fly. What's happening?"

What was happening was a great hatch of large, black stoneflies. This was the first sunny morning in nearly a week of rainy, cloudy weather, and the bugs were taking advantage of it. The nymphs had crawled out of the water onto the top of the tent to complete their emergence in a nice warm spot. Before our eyes, their wing-cases broke open, their wings unfurled, and, after a few seconds, they flew off to nearby bushes. It was quite a sight.

We got dressed in record time, located the fly

▲ ▲ *A fat grayling that liked the stoneflies.*
▲ *Drifting a dry fly.*
▶ *Ready for the release.*

box that contained the stonefly nymphs, and went to work. Fish after fish got suckered into thinking our bugs were real. We could hardly release a fish before we had another on. During the ride home, I learned that Tanya's favorite part of the morning had been knowing the fish-catching "secret" while several people around us were getting skunked.

On this trip, Jodi had also become sold on nymphs. She had decided to alternate using dries and nymphs on one stretch of river I like to call the aqua water. Even though the fish were rising, she was busy proving she could entice them just as well with a peacock-herled zug bug. "Even when they're rising for dry flies, they'll still take nymphs," she marveled. "All I really have to do is get either one in the feeding lane and they'll take it. Boy, am I prepared now."

Jodi was mostly right. Water levels and water clarity both affect graylings' feeding habits, and so, we were about to learn, do the weather and the barometer. A storm was approaching from the nearby mountains as we fished a gorgeous stretch of riffles that day, and the grayling were going crazy! They took dry flies, they took nymphs, they took anything we threw at them. They were actually leaping out of the water for both the naturals and our imitations. In one short stretch of the creek, the group caught and released at least fifty fish in half an hour . . . then, all of a sudden, nothing.

While we weren't looking, the storm that had excited the fish, and that we thought had passed

us by, turned and snuck in behind us. We didn't realize what was happening, but the fish knew. Without warning came a huge clap of thunder and a blast of cold air driving hailstones the size of salt rock at us as we rushed to get out of the water. It had been a great afternoon while it lasted.

Next morning, Maureen carefully sized up the situation, picked her spot next to water flowing out from behind a large rock, and was quietly catching and releasing one grayling after another. Soon she noticed a fellow who'd been unsuccessfully fishing the opposite bank pull in his line and cross the bridge to where we were fishing.

"What fly are you using?" he asked as he approached her, obviously impressed with her accomplishments.

"A nymph," she replied. "My fly of choice."

"Well, I'm not having much luck with dry flies. Guess I should switch, but I don't fish much with nymphs. I really don't know too much about them," he admitted, rummaging around in his fly box.

Maureen patiently picked out from the jumble in his collection some nymphs like those our group had been using successfully. She even gave him one of her split shot and showed him where to place it on his leader. He would have liked for her to give him her fishing spot too, I think, but that was too much to ask. She returned to her catching, and he moved on down the river.

"I felt like I really knew what I was doing," she laughed, as she recounted the incident to her colleagues on the way home. She did.

Bows and Belly Boats

FLOAT TUBING

"Paddle, paddle," the women in the group shouted back and forth. By this point in the afternoon they'd learned that, if they stopped paddling their float tubes when a fish took their fly, they'd lose the fish. So, now, here they were giving one another advice about this thing called float tubing. And doing a very good job of it.

Joan's trout zinged and zoomed around the lake, jumping every once in a while to show us how beautiful it was. For her part, Joan was doing a masterful job of remembering all the pointers about how to play it from a float tube. She swung around as often as necessary so that she would always be facing her catch; she let the fish run but palmed her reel to keep him under control; and she kept her rod tip high to maintain the tension on the fly.

"This is great," she called to the others, who hadn't yet caught a fish. "Just wait till you get one on. It's so much more fun than sitting in a boat."

USING A FLOAT TUBE

A float tube is a personal watercraft that contains a seat and permits an angler wearing chest-high Neoprene waders and swim fins to paddle

◄ *Belly boating in a swarm of bugs.*
▲ *It's a little trickier to land a fish in a float tube.*

around a lake while fishing. Originally referred to as a "belly boat," because it appears to encircle the angler's belly, a float tube requires neither a motor nor paddles. It's the fly fisher's legs that move the craft around. Some related models, called "u" boats, are bulkier than float tubes but easier to get in and out of because they're open in the front instead of round.

It always takes extra time for everyone to get ready to go tubing because of what one has to learn right off the bat. There's extra gear to put on and lots of new information to absorb.

"Sit on the edge of your float tubes and I'll show you how to put on your fins," I tell the first-timers after they've struggled into their waders. "Flippers have to be on tight, and you have to attach the Velcro flipper-keeper around your ankle in case one comes loose. Because the round shape makes it impossible to lean over far enough to reach your feet once you're in the tube, flippers have to be put on first."

Actually getting into the float tube involves more doing than explaining. You either step into the tube, which is tricky with flippers on, or you pull it down over your head. Some women opt for

one method and some for the other. Once in, you must buckle the strap that connects the tube to the seat. That prevents you from sliding out the front. When you've done that, and also donned your life jacket, you're ready to take off.

Launching the float tube requires backing into the water while clutching the handles on the tube as well as the fly rod. The length of the flippers prevents you from walking forward. Upon reaching a depth that is knee deep, you simply sit down and kick off.

"I feel like I'm floating in a donut. You're sure this thing is going to hold me up?" Diane asked, peering down into the depths of the lake.

"Yep, everyone has that question at the beginning," I assured her. "It just takes a little getting used to." After their nerves settled down a bit, we moved on to the next step. "You can only go backwards in a float tube," I told them. "Just point one of your flippers straight down and then push it forward in a 'scooping' motion. Now do the same thing with your other foot. Just keep doing that and you'll be moving. Look back over your shoulder once in a while to make sure you stay on course."

"When you arrive at the spot where you want to fish, you paddle with just one foot so you can turn the tube around and face your target. Then you're ready to cast." I demonstrated while Diane and everyone else overcame those initial moments of anxiety that always plague novice float tubers.

"It's hard to paddle. I'm not getting anywhere,"

B.J. complained. She was a serious scuba diver and was trying to get around with typical swimming motions. B.J. was from California and Diane was from the Southwest. Although both had fly fished before, this was their first time in the float tubes.

"The paddle motion here is different than when you're swimming," I told them all. "Remember, you're sitting upright and not lying prone. Here it's the 'scoop' method that works."

"Oh, I get it now," said Nancy, another first-timer as she extended her leg and then pushed water with her flipper. "It's like riding a bicycle backwards. This is much easier."

They were ready to fish.

FLY FISHING FROM A FLOAT TUBE

It didn't take long. A few minutes of practice adjusting their cast to take into account their sitting position was all they needed. Joan was busy releasing a very active hen fish when the tip of Pauline's rod dipped sharply. While she worked that fish, B.J. also connected. A triple! It was easy to see their confidence increase with every fish. They were hooking, landing, and releasing fish with the skill of seasoned float tubers, calling congratulations on each success, and then proceeding to do it all over again. "Keep your rod tip up," the others yelled. "And paddle," they'd add, if they saw someone had stopped, or, "Palm your reel," as the fish took off.

It was chaos for a while with whoops of laughter, fish jumping, and women paddling

◄ *The tubes, the flippers, the rods, and the reels, just rarin' to go.*
▲ *Carol masters using a net to land the fish from the tube.*

furiously. The fish were beautiful fifteen- and six-teen-inch rainbows, one following the other in rapid succession. Although nobody noticed right then, a pair of velvet-headed black and white common loons watched the show as the tubers tried to avoid one another's tubes and lines.

"Are you sure we're not just catching the same fish over and over again?" someone asked. "These fish all look pretty much alike."

"Well, it's possible," I told them. "Fish are only supposed to have a seven-second memory. I think, however, that they're probably all the same size because they came from the hatchery at the same time."

We'd tied on one of our favorite lake flies—a #8 olive bead head lake leech—and the fish loved it. Some of the males exhibited flaming scarlet cheeks, but just as many, bright and shiny as a new dime, did not. They really did not all look alike.

TUBING IN THE SPRING

In the springtime Alaska's rainbows typically cruise the lake shore. They feed voraciously in the warmer, more comfortable shallows after their long winter under the ice. Others seek out gravelly places in which to mimic the spawning ritual that river fish successfully complete. Those are the places where we look for them first. Rocky points, sandy bottoms beneath overhanging logs or bushes, or pebbled areas next to drop-offs are spots we always try.

This particular weekend, in a howling wind

▲▲ *A spring beauty and a proud tuber.*
▲ *A loon checks out the tubes.*

and rainstorm, we'd driven north from Anchorage to one of our favorite lakes. All of us were worried that the wind would keep us off the water. Still, the group willingly donned rain gear, shouldered their packs and float tubes, and hiked through the dripping and newly leafed out woods to our rented cabin. "Wow, it sure does smell good," somebody remarked as we walked along.

The cabin is really a rustic white wall tent built on a platform with a corrugated plastic roof. It boasts a small propane stove and heater, bunks, and a table with benches. It's cozy and comfortable with a nice deck and picnic table and, on a clear day, a stunning view of Mount McKinley, North America's highest peak. It sits right on the lake.

By the time we got settled in and re-inflated the tubes, the wind had calmed and the rain had settled down to just sprinkles. We were eager to get going.

Fish were roiling right next to the bank at the foot of the hill below the cabin, so that's where we started. It was amazing how easily we could see them and how totally unconcerned they were about us. At times their backs even protruded out of the water. We paddled out, turned our tubes and cast back toward shore. As we stripped our nymph patterns out into deeper water, fish after fish grabbed them.

"Set the hook well and then paddle back into deeper water," I advised Diane, as a very aggressive fish took her hare's ear nymph. "That way you won't spook the other cruisers." She moved quickly out of range, played, netted, and released her fish, then was back for more in just a few minutes.

"When I got him in, that fish measured seventeen inches. That's much bigger than he'd looked to me in the water," she told the others. "So, don't hesitate to cast to ones that you think don't look very big." She followed her own advice and quickly landed another fish as long as her first.

Diane and her husband own their own company. She'd been under a lot of pressure and needing a vacation. So, on the spur of the moment, she'd called me up, packed her bag, and gotten on a plane.

"This is a perfect stress reliever," she commented. "I haven't thought about work once today."

That evening, when the lake surface gleamed with shafts of Alaska's long spring light, we just couldn't bring ourselves to head for the sleeping bags. So back into the tubes we went. We found fish hovering in the drop-off next to the shallows of a nearby island, drifting back and forth between warmth and the safety of deeper water. A small, black woolly bugger, stripped in slowly through the shallows and then permitted to sink, resulted in lots of fish for this bunch.

Between them, Pauline and Nancy, fishing side by side on one end of the island, landed fifteen large fish in an hour, and the others weren't far behind.

▲ *Keeping a tight line in the tube.*

We finally returned to the cabin, but still weren't ready to sleep. Instead, we made a cup of tea (knowing full well it would mean a visit to the outhouse during the night) and sat dreaming on the lakeshore taking in the haunting calls of the loons and the splendor of the mountain bathed in alpenglow.

TUBING IN THE SUMMER

During the summer months, many of the largest fish in the lakes retreat to cooler water fifteen to twenty feet deep. So, we trade our floating lines for sink tips and troll for them there.

"Here we go," Christine announced, five minutes after we'd launched our tubes this Fourth of July weekend. For emphasis, a fat and energetic rainbow launched itself into the air between her tube and mine.

No problem. Christine had the routine down perfectly: lift the rod tip to set the hook, paddle backwards to keep a tight line, and let the line slide out slowly until the fish is on the reel. Then let it play, and reel when it rests. Christine float tubes quite often and is extremely good at feeling the take, patiently playing the fish, and never losing her cool.

This fish proved to be a gorgeous eighteen-inch hen so silvery that hardly a blush of pink showed along her lateral line or on her gill plates. Everyone gathered around while we had a lesson on catch and release from a float tube. Christine slowly paddled with just one foot, turning her

tube in a circle and creating a current into which she could point the fish's nose. The maneuver ensured that water flowed through its gills and revived it. The lake's resident eagle watched intently from a nearby spruce ready to quickly pick up any fish that wasn't released successfully.

The entire morning went like that. Hook a fish, play a fish, release a fish, watch the loons. It was a great start to a weekend filled with healthy, gleaming fish.

That night we had rain, and the next morning a steady drizzle fell amidst the fog—perfect fishing weather!

"Got him," Helen hollered, as her rod tip dipped sharply and a fish jumped three feet out of the water. Helen was a somewhat unusual fly fisher. All her previous fishing experience had been using a subsistence net in the Alaska Native community where she grew up. Now she was finding out just how much fun sport fishing can be, and she wasn't being quiet about it.

We counted nine jumps on Helen's fish before she finally landed it. Within three casts after the release, she had another one and then quickly a third. It was her spot. Soon everyone else was hooking up too. These fish were only a mere fourteen inches but as eager and active as their larger cousins from the day before.

Suddenly, one of the loons fishing nearby decided that a fish that Elaine was playing looked better than what he was catching, and he came over to join us. Before she could react, he grabbed

Bows and Belly Boats

her fish in his beak and proceeded to try to pull it off her line. He was very persistent!

"What do I do?" she cried. "I don't want to be catching a loon."

"Just give the fish a good yank and see if you can pull it away from him," I suggested.

That worked, but as she tried to quickly reel it in, the loon made another lunge. This time he missed. He seemed to realize that it was tethered and couldn't get away. Even though he'd been unsuccessful, he continued to circle her tube for a few minutes.

The fish's skin was marked by the loon's beak, and it probably was pretty traumatized. Nevertheless, it swam away strongly when Elaine released it.

"Whew," Elaine commented, "that was quite an experience." She'd certainly never encountered anything like this where she was from in the Midwest. "I never thought I'd get a chance to play with a loon while I was fishing," she added.

Most people must settle for recalling pictures of loons they've seen or the forlorn wail they've heard in the distance. They never get to listen to or view this very special lake-dweller up close. We've been luckier. Because they are so quiet, float tubes enable us to get a first-hand look at these magnificent birds, seeing loon behavior that most people never see, and listening to loon talk that most people never hear.

This particular day, while the loons distracted us, a brute of a fish came calling. Really large rain-

◄ Not a ripple, not even a breeze, just fish and summer fireweed. A great stress reliever.
▲ A lovely rainbow and her glistening reflection.

bows tend to hit a trolled fly and head straight to the depths of the lake. And that's what this one did. He never surfaced, never jumped, and made none of the straight out runs that our other fish had demonstrated. Instead, Jeannie's rod just stayed bent downward.

"He won't break my rod, will he?" she asked.

"I don't think so. Just hold on and keep paddling," I replied. "You'll need to be sure you maintain the tension on the line in case he turns and swims toward you. Your rod should be fine."

57

It was about as long a contest as you'd expect from a twenty-four-inch fish that has forty feet of depth to use against you. The fish just stayed deep, occasionally pulling Jeannie's tube around after him. It seemed like he would never get tired.

"He's spectacular," Jeannie exclaimed, when he finally gave up and came to hand. And he was. So spectacular, in fact, that I couldn't get him into the landing net. I took the opportunity to show her how to carefully tail him and release the tension on her line so we could remove the hook.

This fish was not only long, he was also in prime condition, a deep-bodied buck with rose-colored cheeks. The old reliable brown and black woolly bugger fly had done it again.

After that, our shore lunch was something of a letdown, but we needed the sustenance for what was to come. Shortly after getting back into our tubes, we saw fish rising in a small cove near us, and we headed there to investigate. The water had been covered with tiny midges all morning, but there'd been no fish rising. Mayflies, however, were causing all the excitement now. Although we weren't able to match that hatch exactly, a #12 yellow soft-hackle, fished just below the surface, did the trick.

These fish turned out to be stocked, land-locked silver salmon and not the rainbows we had been catching. They weren't as big, but there were so many of them, they were just as much fun. As quickly as we delivered the fly, we'd have a hook-up. All the rods were bent with fish all the time.

▲ *This one took some time to land.*

Many of the fish were in the ten- to twelve-inch range, but quite a few fourteen- and fifteen-inchers cooperated just as eagerly. It was a great opportunity to practice catch and release from a tube.

When Christine's perfect loop delivered her fly, there'd be a momentary hesitation, and then the line would come tight. It happened with uncanny regularity. "This is almost too easy," she laughed. A loon pair nearby agreed. They were fishing as successfully as we were. They dove and surfaced and dove again right next to us emerging with small, wriggling fish in their beaks that they quickly fed to their two begging chicks.

None of us had ever seen anything like the underwater show they put on. Because of the clarity of the water, we had front row seats. The speed and agility of the huge birds in their element was incredible. They dove and turned with unbelievable dexterity, and then silently surfaced with barely a ripple, glistening beads of water dripping from their velvet heads.

Jeannie had brought a fish close to her tube and was attempting to land it when she suddenly felt something brush her leg. We looked down into the water to see one of the loons streaking upwards toward her fish. Thinking fast, she quickly rotated her tube and moved the fish out of the way. Nevertheless, the loon's attempt to grab a fish so close to a tube was amazing. These great birds are a never-ending source of delight for us as we paddle Alaska's lakes.

EQUIPMENT AND FLIES FOR
SPRING AND SUMMER TUBING

The best fly rods for float tubing are nine feet long. Shorter rods are difficult to cast from the sitting position. We use primarily 5-weight rods, although, when the wind isn't a factor, a 4-weight rod can make lake fishing extra enjoyable. Some people advocate using even lighter weight rods, but the risk of having to play a fish so long that it cannot be revived makes me recommend and use only the 4- or 5-weights.

Whatever the reel, a strong drag is necessary for the unexpected large fish often encountered in Alaska's lakes. That reel needs to be equipped with two spools, one holding a weight-forward floating line for spring fishing and one holding a sinking-tip line for trolling. My favorite sinking-tip line for lake fishing is a twenty-four-foot, 100-grain lead-core line.

Wet fly fishing is often more reliable on many of Alaska's lakes in the summer. Nymphs, leeches, and small bait fish imitations seem to take most of the big fish, although occasionally we see some dry fly action. We always have some midge and caddis imitations on hand, just in case. As happened this particular day, we also have success with the yellow or olive soft-hackle patterns.

Our most productive flies in the spring are typically a black, brown, olive, or purple #8 or #10 bead-head lake leech, the same size and color woolly buggers, or any number of different smolt imitations also in 8 or 10. Both olive and tan gold-

▲▲ *Hooked by the net.*
▲ *Lake leeches, woolly buggers and more.*

ribbed hare's ear nymphs in #10 or #12 also take lots of fish.

In the summer, we're apt to do more trolling. For that, the brown/black woolly bugger on a #6 or #8 hook is the hands-down favorite on nearly every lake we fish. The bead-head lake leech runs a close second.

LAKE FLY FISHING AND WILDLIFE WATCHING

Often, when float tubing, it's hard to concentrate on fishing because there's so much wildlife activity going on. One fine spring morning, a mature bald eagle scouted the lake for baby ducks and birds with which to feed her young. Gulls and terns courted and squawked all around us. The swallows appeared en masse when the morning midge hatch began, their swoops and dives reminiscent of a ballet. Then, as we rounded a small point of land, we were amazed to see a pair of sand-hill cranes resting on the shore of the lake. We stopped paddling immediately and just watched as they nonchalantly rose up and marched off into the trees. Since they nest farther north, the cranes are only temporary visitors to the lakes we float tube.

Summer float tubing gives us an opportunity for great loon-watching. Many of the lakes we fish host a breeding pair of common loons. One, and sometimes two, fluffy gray chicks are born around the Fourth of July and take to the water immediately with their black and white speckled parents. Some of the most endearing sights of loons are

Often the loons surface so close we can see their carmine eyes, pitch black heads, and checkered necklace. They appear to have no fear of the float tubes. In fact, I think they're curious about us and our floating contraptions. On more than one occasion, they've approached almost to the tip of a fly rod and sat preening and vocalizing. They seem to love it when we try to call back to them in a less-than-perfect imitation. We just don't speak loon very well.

One morning, as we sat casting and wildlife watching, a large, dark fish greeted Elaine. Thinking she was hung up on some of the debris at the lakeshore, she tugged carefully on her fly. Instead of coming lose, though, her woolly bugger took off, squarely in the jaw of a giant rainbow.

"He's practically towing me around," she said. "I don't know if I can control him." Back and forth he ran with Elaine patiently reeling in, letting him run, and reeling in again. "Careful, careful," I heard her murmur to herself. "Don't rush him."

"How long does this usually take?" she finally asked. "I'm getting tired." After about eight sizzling runs and as many spectacular jumps, we thought the fish must be tiring too. Elaine began to work him toward the tube for release, and I had the net ready. He was having none of it, though, diving for the bottom every time we got him to the surface. One last time, she eased him in. The top of his tail protruded at least two inches out of the water. This was one big fish. Touching him was not to be, however.

those where one or two tiny, bright-eyed little heads peek out from under the folded wings of a parent bird who is providing warmth, safety, and a free ride for the fledglings.

▲ *A tubing strategy session.*

With a shake of his massive head, he threw the hook and quickly returned to the depths of the lake just as Elaine reached to tail him.

"On no," she cried. "I thought I had him for sure." I'm surprised she didn't break into tears. What a disappointment!

"Okay, so how big do you think he was?" she demanded to know after a few breathless seconds.

"Probably the largest rainbow I've ever seen in this lake," I replied. "Twenty-six or twenty-seven inches long." No kidding.

It took a while before we could resume fishing after an experience like that.

"What did it feel like?" "Did you worry your rod would break?" "Was that the biggest fish you've ever caught on a fly rod?" Question after question came at Elaine, whose hands were still shaking five minutes later.

▲ *A pod of fish and some fly fishers, both taking advantage of a hatch.*

"That fish might always be the 'one that got away' for me," she said mournfully.

And she was right. Any smaller fish right then might have been anti-climactic. Thank goodness another marvelous phenomenon took place instead. As we paddled toward the cabin for lunch, a pair of pearl-white swans suddenly appeared overhead. Homeward bound, they were on course to their summer nesting grounds in western Alaska. They flew so low to the water we could hear their squawking calls and the swoosh of their mighty wings. We almost flipped over our tubes as we bent backwards to watch them. We breathlessly hoped they might land to rest on the lake, but they ascended over the treetops and flew on toward the horizon. Seeing them in flight was a rare treat. Seeing them while tubing an Alaskan lake was even better.

Sockeye Stalking

THE BROOKS RIVER

Blondes, brunettes, and redheads of the two-legged variety all go fly fishing. They come from all walks of life and from every age group. Seventeen or seventy, they have one thing in common—a love of the outdoors and the magic of the moment when they shout "got him!"

Well, in Alaska, blonde, brunette, and brown anglers of the four-legged variety also abound. Those infamous fishers are the bears. As salmon enter Alaska's rivers beginning in late spring, and continue through summer and into early fall, they are as apt to be fishing as we are. The blondies and brownies of that species become as much a part of the focus for our groups on the Brooks River as the sockeye (or "red") salmon. We watch intently for these large residents and vacate the fishing holes whenever they appear.

"Bear upriver on the other side," Leslie shouted, one sunny afternoon as we stood casting on the bank. The large, chocolate brown boar known as Hershey Bar had emerged from the willows just above one of our favorite fishing holes. His huge head swung back and forth scanning the river for signs of salmon. We quickly pulled in our fly lines and backed away from the water to give him plenty of room.

◄ *We watch intently for the bears, and vacate the fishing hole when they appear.*
▲ *Checking the scene before starting to fish.*

Leslie, a U.S. Fish and Wildlife administrator and an experienced Alaskan outdoorswoman, was well acquainted with these large Alaska residents. She had attended our Talstar Lodge fly fishing school for women the previous year and knew that respecting the bear's space was more important than continuing to fish.

"Stay together and don't run," I advised the group, as we stood well back on the bank and held our breath waiting to see what Hershey Bar would do. Not many fish were present, thank goodness, and finally he lumbered on past us down toward the lake.

We all resumed fishing after old "candy bar" had passed safely, but we kept a watchful eye for his return or for a visit from one of his cohorts. And that wasn't long in coming. About ten minutes later, one of the smaller bears (referred to as "teenagers" by National Park Service rangers who patrol the area) came crashing right down the middle of the river, driving a school of salmon in front of him. Like a cat pouncing on a mouse, he leapt and dove right into the swirling hoard of fish spraying water far and wide. Although he was paying no attention to us, once again we moved

out of the water and watched while he played with his food.

He wasn't very experienced at catching fish, but finally managed to get his teeth and his claws around a fine, chubby sockeye specimen that had jumped out of the water to avoid him and lay flopping on the bank.

With the fish wriggling in his jaws, the young bear quickly looked around to make sure a bigger bear wasn't nearby to snatch it away. Then he furtively stole into the high grass for his lunch. Soon he was back searching frantically for another fish on the beach, not able to figure out why there wasn't another where he had "caught" the first. Finally, he, too, wandered off, and then it was our turn.

Our adolescent friend had stirred up the fish quite nicely. They were more than eager to take our flies. The river bend we call the "meat hole" was now full of salmon, and it was just a matter of getting our flies to the correct depth on the right drift to get a hook-up.

"Fish on," Tanya cried, as a glistening torpedo shot into the air and splashed back into the river. She forgot that she had to set the hook a couple of times in a salmon's bony mouth, however, so pretty soon it was "fish off." But the next time, she remembered. Patti and Shawn, who were fishing below her, quickly reeled in their lines to avoid tangling her fish, and we all settled down to watch the show.

There's something primeval about the battle

between people and fish. On a fly rod it's a true test of intellect over power. (Anyone who doubts that a eight-pound salmon has the strength to out-fight a human hasn't fished for one on a fly rod.)

"There's so much to remember," Tanya wailed as the group kept reminding her to let him run, to palm her reel, and to keep her rod tip up to maintain tension on the fly. All the while the fish was doing a great job of alternately holding in the current or streaking downstream to keep Tanya constantly on her toes.

A project manager for a large construction company in Alaska, Tanya had fished with my groups before. Previously, she targeted only rainbows and Arctic grayling, but she'd recently decided to move up to fishing for the big guys. Even though these larger fish were more challenging to her, she was now able to make good use of the lessons she'd learned on other fish. She knew to let the fish run and to reel when it rested.

"Don't lose him now," Patti cautioned, as Tanya carefully played the tiring fish closer and closer into shore.

"Tail him, Pudge, tail him," they yelled, just as I grabbed the fish in front of its tail to end the encounter. Since anglers are prohibited from putting a fish on the bank because the smell attracts bears, I dispatched the fish with a quick rap on its head right in the water. Then Tanya knelt down for the obligatory picture of her first sockeye.

"Yahoo," screamed Shawn. "Our first fish of

◄▲ *"Fish On," Tanya cried.*
◄ *Never mind my hat, just save the fish.*
▲▲ *Saying goodbye.*
▲ *The first fish of the afternoon.*

the afternoon." She was as excited about Tanya's fish as if she'd caught it herself. Shawn, an engineer from Colorado, was Tanya's cousin, and this was their first fishing trip together. Shawn's previous conquests had been small rainbows in the Rockies. Now the cousins were fishing for the largest fish they'd ever sought. "Their" fish was a beauty. Fresh and silvery, it was quite a prize, in spite of its long trip from the ocean up the Naknek River and across Naknek Lake to Brooks.

Although Tanya had been successful, her work wasn't done. Under park service rules, if she intended to keep this fish, she had to get it back to the lodge immediately to avoid attracting the bears. So, while she placed her fish in the regulation plastic bag and hiked back to the lodge with it, the rest of the group kept fishing. Shawn and Jane hooked up almost simultaneously.

"I didn't feel a hit," said Jane. "My fly just stopped."

"Well, I felt mine," Shawn hollered, "and look at him go."

Both rods were bent and both fish were taking out line quickly. Just like their captors, the fish fought side by side in the current downriver of us.

"Slow them down by palming your reels," I reminded. "Press up on the spool from underneath with the flat of your hand." In their excitement they'd forgotten one of the requirements of playing salmon on a fly rod. But they quickly recovered, and the struggle to get the fish to the bank was underway.

"Keep your rod tip pointed at your fish, and don't reel while the fish is running. Just palm." I told them. "Reel only when the fish rests."

"It's working," Shawn, said. "He's coming in."

Well, so did Jane's, and the next thing we knew, both fish were coming in simultaneously—all wound up together. We tried separating the fish by having Jane lower her rod while Shawn lifted hers, and by having the two of them reel exactly alike to see if we might just get the fish in together, but nothing worked. Finally the inevitable happened. Both fish were gone. Shawn's had thrown the hook, and Jane's had broken the leader. They consoled each other even as they recounted just how exciting it had all been to their cheering section, Leslie and Patti.

Actually, it was just as well we didn't land the fish together. We'd have had a difficult time dealing with them and following Park Service rules to get them both into plastic bags without placing either of them on the bank where their smell might have lingered.

"Wait till we tell Tanya about our double," they said, returning to their fishing. It was amazing to watch this group. Tanya and Shawn may have known each other previously, but even though Patti and Jane were both real estate agents from Anchorage, they'd never become acquainted. No one in the group had ever met Leslie, but you'd have thought they had all known each other for years, they were having such a great time together.

▲ *Sockeye attempt to leap Brooks falls.*

THE BROOKS RIVER

The world-famous Brooks River, where we and the bears stalked sockeye, is in Katmai National Park, southwest of Anchorage across Cook Inlet. The three-mile river drains Brooks Lake into Naknek Lake, one of the five largest lakes in Alaska.

The river is the main corridor for the passage of huge numbers of sockeye salmon to their spawning grounds, and bears as well as people know about it. The swift, boulder-strewn waters of the upper river change to more classic runs and riffles below an eight-foot high waterfall that bisects the river at its midway point. This natural barrier concentrates fish below it in a bathtub-like plunge pool, providing some easy pickings for the bears. Until they visit the area, few people associate the profusion of bears with the waterfall.

In order to progress upriver to their spawning grounds, the salmon have no choice but to jump the falls. So, they congregate in the pool at the base of the cascading water in huge numbers to attempt the leap again and again. The bears wait for them both in the pool and atop the falls.

The Brooks River spectacle is epitomized by pictures of a huge brown bear standing atop the surging waterfall with open jaws that are about to snap closed on a leaping sockeye salmon. This concentration of brown bears during the salmon runs makes Brooks River and Brooks Lodge one of Alaska's most popular wilderness attractions.

Sockeye Stalking

THE BEARS

As many as forty bears converge along the Brooks River in mid-July at the height of the salmon run. Brooks' bears are all brownies, even

▲ Standing atop the falls, a bear awaits the fish while we watch from the safety of the platform.

though some may have a distinct blond coloration. Many are identifiable year after year. "Diver" was a gargantuan old bear covered with battle scars. Last sighted in 2001, he liked to

67

Diver year after year or checking on whether an injured bear from a previous year has made it through the winter.

We take the mile-long hike to Brooks Falls several times during our annual trip to see the bears fishing. Snarling and battling for the choicest spots to catch jumping sockeye in mid-air, the bears fish from rock outcroppings atop the falls that jut forth into the cascading water. As we watch, other bears dip their heads into the water and grab a fish out of the boiling mass in the plunge pool. Needless to say, the largest bears get the best spots. Younger bears often have to settle for the leavings of their elders until they perfect their fishing skills.

One year we were privileged to observe two sows with their spring cubs. One mom had twin babies and the other had a single dark fur-ball following alongside. The little ones have the appearance of toy teddy bears, and it is difficult to imagine the 800-pound behemoths they can become if they live to adulthood. The female bears are in a particularly difficult situation. They must fish to feed themselves and their cubs while at the same time standing guard to protect their offspring from the large boars that will eat such small morsels for a snack if they get the chance.

For centuries sows have taught their cubs that the falls is an impediment to fish passage and, as such, presents a unique feeding opportunity. Year after year, they all come to take advantage of it. Before and after the salmon runs, the bears

snorkel for salmon in the lake and below the falls and was the dominant male at the falls for many summers. He's still so famous that trading cards at the visitor center carry his pictures in various poses. Then, of course, the formidable Hershey Bar often makes an appearance, displaying a gangster-like intimidation of all the other bears.

The park service discourages naming the bears to keep people from thinking of them as pets. That doesn't stop us long-time visitors from asking about and keeping our eyes peeled for

▲ *Sows teach their cubs about fishing the Brooks River.*

inhabit other areas, often many miles distant. Exactly how they know when the salmon are in the river and when to travel to Brooks is one of the great mysteries of life that we humans ponder as we watch the show from the safety of the observation platform.

THE NATIONAL PARK AND ITS RULES

The National Park Service maintains a headquarters near Brooks Lodge. It focuses on preventing problems between people and bears. Therefore, it imposes certain requirements on all visitors. Whether you come to fish or just to view the bears, you're required to visit the park service building immediately upon disembarking from the float plane that brought you from the town of King Salmon, a twenty-minute flight away.

At the headquarters, visitors must watch a video about how to behave around the bears and then wear a button proclaiming that they've seen it. The video reminds people not to carry food of any sort while fishing or walking around the area, to make loud noise at all times, and never to run when a bear approaches. During the orientation, anglers learn the park's special fishing rules.

Fishing regulations permit each angler to keep only one salmon per day. Since the 1999 fishing season, that fish must have been caught below the bridge that spans the river just before it enters Naknek Lake. Any fish that is kept may not be placed on the bank or cleaned on the river. It must be deposited whole in the regulation plastic bag

▲ *The fish are right over there. I can hear'em.*

and taken immediately to the freezer at the lodge, as Tanya did. After returning to the river, the successful angler may continue to fish for salmon, but must practice catch and release for the rest of the day.

If playing a fish when a bear appears, we're required to break the fish off immediately or even cut the line to avoid having the bear associate a splashing fish with people. Needless to say, those rules make for some heart-pounding encounters on the river. We follow the rules religiously and have never had a problem. We've also learned the value of having a spare fly line along, however. One year we were forced to sever a line to separate a woman from her fish when a bear approached.

That particular morning we'd decided to fish along the shore of the lake where the river enters. Unless the water is high, there's a long, open beach with easy casting that enables us to intercept fish as they move up from the lake. It had been a good morning, with lots of fish. As the others headed back to the lodge, Gail asked if she could fish just a little longer. She was still working on sensing the slight line hesitation that indicates a sockeye hook-up and wanted some more practice.

She was happily doing battle with a nice fish when a young bear topped a small wooded hill down the beach. At that time he was well beyond the fifty yards distance that the park service requires between people and bears, but I suspected he'd head our way before long.

"We'd better break the fish off," I told Gail.

▲▲ *Landing a Brooks River rainbow.*

▲ *Fish-love!*

"There's a bear coming. Try pulling the line tight and then quickly letting go." Often, creating slack quickly causes the fly to drop out of the fish's mouth. It didn't work this time.

Although Gail had plenty of practice with the technique of pointing the rod tip right at the fish and giving a sharp, backward tug to yank the fly out, that didn't work either. "Oh, no," she whispered. "I'll bet I tied on too heavy a leader the last time and now I can't break it when I need to."

The bear was meandering along down the beach. It was padding through small rivulets of water looking for fish remains, totally unconcerned with us. Nevertheless, I was getting nervous.

"Take my rod," I told her, "and give me yours. I'll see if I can break off the fish." As a glanced up I noticed that the bear had stopped. His attention had switched to the river channel where the fish struggled at the end of Gail's line. He wasn't running, just alert.

Well, Gail had used too heavy leader material for her tippet and it wasn't about to separate. She'd done such a good job of setting the hook that it wasn't coming out either. I couldn't get the fish off, and I couldn't get at my clippers to cut the line.

The bear was starting toward us now. Thank goodness the fish wasn't splashing. Nevertheless, as the bear got nearer, he was bound to notice it. It's crucial that bears not learn to associate fish with people, or they can become a real nuisance.

"We should talk to the bear," I told Gail, "and

tell it we're leaving. But, don't run. And, don't make eye contact. Bears take that as confrontation."

As Gail and I stepped rapidly backwards, calling "goodbye-bear" over and over, I was pulling line off her reel as fast as I could. That snake of bright yellow, lying along the beach between us and the bear, got longer and longer as we got farther away.

Luckily, an angler just walking out onto the beach noticed our plight. By this time all ninety feet of fly line and probably twenty yards of line-backing were decorating the beach. Our savior quickly severed the backing with his knife and we all paused to let our hearts slow down.

Eventually the bear splashed into the water, clamped his jaws around the fish, and took off back down the beach and over the little hill where he'd come from. Ten minutes later, a park ranger and I collected the line off the beach. We were amazed to notice that the hook, which earlier had been so firmly lodged in the fish, was still attached to the end of the line.

Sometimes it seems as though there are too many rules at Brooks, but each one has an important purpose. Over many years, the park service has learned how to minimize people-bear encounters so we can enjoy the setting without threatening its true inhabitants. Brooks is the bears' home, after all. We're just visitors. The rules are for the visitors.

Even if all fishing were restricted to catch and release, we'd still go back to Brooks. The place has

▲ *Tying on a fly just right.*
▶ *Watching bears from the lower platform.*

Just like the bears, we know that when the reds are "in," the fishing can be awesome. Shawn, Jane, Leslie, and Tanya caught and released easily one hundred fifty fish one afternoon when they found themselves in the middle of a huge school of salmon moving up a small channel in the river. Patti hadn't felt well and had opted for a nap in the cabin. If only she had known.

We could see the wall of dark backs and the line of fish wakes as the school approached. Talk about breathless anticipation! Some fish tried to turn back upon seeing us but met others coming at them from behind. Quickly, the water turned to a frothing, swirling frenzy of fish, and it was pandemonium. Fish bumped into each other and into us, leaped out of the water when there was no room for them to swim, and tried their best to get away from the chaos. All four rods were hooked up all the time!

"I don't believe this," Shawn said. "I've read about the runs of salmon, but this is unbelievable. I've never seen or caught so many fish, or such big fish, in my life."

"And you probably never will again," Tanya added.

"I'm getting so tired I want to stop, but I can't." Jane announced. "This is a once in a life-time opportunity, and I don't want to miss a second of it. Patti is going to really be sick when we tell her what she missed."

"Just enjoy it while it lasts," I told them.

By this time these women were working

an indescribable magnetism that cannot be denied. There is no place like it in the world.

THE FISH AND THE FISHING

"Reds," or "bluebacks," as sockeye salmon are often called, weigh about eight pounds on average in most of Alaska's rivers. Only pink, or "humpy," salmon are smaller. Chinook, or "king" salmon are the largest Pacific salmon, with chum and silver salmon running neck and neck for second place. In their spawning colors, sockeyes' bodies are ketchup-red while their heads turn a bright Christmas-green. Like all salmon, males are larger than females and develop the distinctive hook-nose profile.

▲ *A spawning red salmon in all her glory.*
▶ ▲ *This is the fly that will hook that fish.*
▶ *The right rod, the right reel and the right fly.*

together well. They timed their casts to avoid tangling each other, ducked under someone else's bent rod to play their fish, shared flies, and helped release one another's fish. We could hardly work fast enough releasing fish or re-rigging from those that broke off. Tourists stood on the bank marveling at the spectacle. These fish, so famous for refusing to take a fly, were hitting our fuscia and chartreuse fish-candy flies as fast as we could present them.

Finally, after almost two hours of non-stop fishing, the brouhaha was over. The river quieted. We retreated to rest our weary arms and celebrate our success over a glass of wine and many a congratulatory comment from others at the lodge. On only a couple of other occasions in all my years fishing at Brooks have I seen such a show.

THE FLIES, THE GEAR, AND THE TECHNIQUE

Reds may not be the largest of Alaska's salmon, but many anglers find them to be the most fun on a fly rod. Pound for pound they offer the fly angler sizzling runs and amazing power. In spite of what happened to us on that incredible afternoon, reds really are notoriously difficult to catch on a fly.

Most experts believe the sockeyes' reluctance to take a fly results from their feeding habits as juveniles. Zooplankton, filtered from the water, is one of the primary food sources for young sockeye in fresh water. So, as the thinking goes, because baby sockeye didn't need to chase their

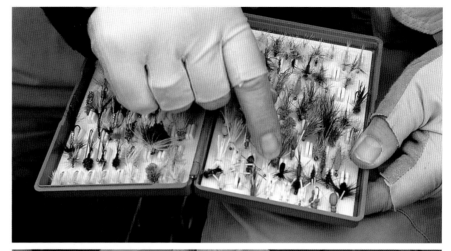

food, they didn't develop as strong a predatory sense as other fish. Besides, plankton are virtually impossible to imitate with a fly.

Luckily, the fly hardly matters in fishing for sockeye. Instead, the trick is to have a sparse fly right at the mouth level of the fish in the water column. That's easier said than done, though. Success usually involves getting the fly to the right depth with either a sink-tip line or split-shot on the leader, or both, depending on the speed and depth of the water. Constant adjustment of leader length and split-shot placement are required to keep the fly floating above the weight at just the right level for consistent hook-ups.

Our favorite fly for reds is a simple one called "fish candy." It is a fluff of bright-colored crystal chenille on either a weighted or un-weighted hook, depending on the particular stretch of water. Other flies we use are a silver-bodied, orange and black-winged pattern, called a sockeye orange, or a red yarn and flashabou mix called the lemon fly, all on a #6 salmon/steelhead hook. Sometimes it's even possible to catch reds on a bare hook, but we're too wedded to the traditional flies so we seldom try it.

We fish for sockeye with 9-foot, 8-weight fly rods. The heavier rod helps in casting sink tip lines or heavier flies in a wind and enables the fly fisher to land a fish more quickly in bear country.

We rig a leader on an 8-weight with a butt section of 10- or 12-pound test monofilament line with an 8-pound tippet. Even though we'll lose an

▲▲ *Magnifiers help with tying the small flies.*
▲ *Hooked right in the mouth.*

occasional fish this way, heavier leaders can prevent us from breaking a fish off easily when a bear appears on the scene, as Gail found out.

Since the Brooks River boasts trophy rainbow trout and Arctic grayling as well as sockeye salmon, we also take 9-foot, 5-weight rods. On some trips, trout and grayling provide most of the action if the salmon runs are late.

ONLY AT BROOKS

That incomparable afternoon when we had such amazing fishing was definitely one to remember. Often, though, it's the 5 a.m. fishing that is the highlight of the Brooks River trip. The river is generally misty and serene in the early hours, with the fish eager for the fight after a night of rest. Generally, we are so entranced by the peace and solitude, we either fish the catch-and-release section of the river or just put all our fish back rather than leaving the river to take our catch to the lodge's freezer.

There's rarely a sound as someone plays a fish. No one wants to break the spell. Once in a while, however, something very special intrudes upon the silence: bagpipe music.

On one such morning, as the haunting strains of "Amazing Grace" drifted over the quiet river, someone said, "I'd never have believed you if you'd told me this would happen. Nowhere else but in Alaska could I be in this gorgeous spot catching salmon to the sounds of the highlands."

But happen it does many mornings when

Rick, the bagpiper, greets the dawn with his pipes. Rick is one of a group of anglers who call themselves the Hairy Dogs. They fish at Brooks every year the same time we do, and we've become friends. Rick's music suits this special river perfectly. Surely, the bears enjoy it too.

Although we've never seen the bears as entranced by Rick's music as we are, we've seen them in other bear-human encounters. We've met them face to face coming up the hill from opposite sides on our hike to the falls; we've had them amble in behind us from protective bushes; and we've seen them passing through the camp as we emerge from our cabin in the early morning. We're always alert, we always respect their space, and we always come away in awe of such a magnificent creature.

At dinner one night, while we were savoring the ever-present brownies (the dessert kind), someone suddenly hollered, "Bear in camp." That brownie was right outside the dining room window! So, the dining room manager, all one hundred pounds of her, stepped out onto the back porch, clapped her hands loudly and yelled, "Bad bear, you know you're not supposed to be in the camp."

Before our very eyes 1,000 pounds of carnivore became an obedient puppy dog. He put his head down, turned around, and slunk away back to the river, well chastised by the big boss of the lodge!

"Only in Alaska," someone remarked.

"And only at Brooks," someone else replied.

▲ *California woman meets Alaska sockeye salmon.*

Chasing Char

THE ANIAK RIVER

I don't believe it. This fish has pink spots," Carolyn announced to the rest of the group. "Come quick and look. It's absolutely gorgeous."

"Pink spots?" Ruth asked. "I thought trout had black spots. What kind of a fish is this?"

Until then, these women had been catching mostly rainbows and a few Arctic grayling with their small egg-imitation flies. They weren't expecting anything else and rushed over to get a glimpse of Carolyn's sleek twenty-inch fish. No wonder they were surprised by this lovely specimen of char. It did, indeed, have large rosy spots along its gunmetal gray sides. The group watched as Carolyn gently removed the hook and held the fish nose-first into the current until it darted away.

Carolyn, a retired California lawyer in her seventies, and Ruth, a thirty-something library administrator, had ended up as tent-mates on this wilderness trip and quickly became fast friends. Although Ruth was the more experienced fly angler initially, Carolyn was catching up. "I started fly fishing rather late in life," Carolyn remarked, "and now I'm fishing as much as I can to make up for it."

"Rainbows and Arctic grayling aren't the only

◀ *A school of Dollies just waiting for the salmon to lay eggs.*
▲ *Solitude on a pristine Alaska stream.*

fish that feed on salmon eggs when they're available," I told them. "Dolly Varden and Arctic char also take advantage of all the food that spawning salmon provide. You can easily tell the difference between trout and char by the color of the spots. Trout have black spots, and char have pink or light spots. You're going to be seeing a lot more char while we're out here. If you think this one is beautiful, just wait."

FISH OF THE RAINBOW

A fall char, resplendent in spawning colors, is one of the most spectacularly painted of all freshwater fish. Displaying a color scheme ablaze with the glow of a flaming sunrise, they possess beauty unmatched by any other northern species, except, perhaps, for their cousins the brook trout. Often referred to as the "lipstick fish," both male and female char sport lips as bright as their bodies during this time. They look as if they've just returned from a trip to the beauty products counter.

Native Alaskans refer to char as Akalukpik, or fish of the rainbow. Legend has it that the fish descended to the rivers from the sky and passed

▲▲ *Dolly Varden char just beginning to sport her spawning colors.*
▲ *A male Dolly Varden brilliant in his spawning colors*

through a rainbow as they did so, getting painted with its brilliant colors in the process. The word char is also thought to derive from the Gaelic word "charr" that refers to a blood-red color. Although the coloration of char can vary with location and age, typically they exhibit light spots on a dark background in contrast to trout, which display just the opposite. Char also have smaller scales than trout.

Two kinds of char roam the rivers in Alaska—the Arctic char and the Dolly Varden char. "Dollies," as they are called, reportedly were named for a character in a Charles Dickens novel who wore a particularly colorful dress. Fisheries biologists are just beginning to explore the physiological differences between Dollies and Arctic char and their interrelationships as species or sub-species. These scientists believe that, at least in northern Alaska, Dolly Varden generally spawn and winter over in rivers, while Arctic char do so in lakes. Of the two, Dollies are the anadromous species.

Back when Alaska was a territory, Dollies were vilified. Because they were thought to eat so many salmon eggs that they posed a risk to that species, the federal government imposed a bounty of 2.5 cents for every Dolly Varden tail turned in during the 1930s. Later, studies proved that char posed no threat to healthy salmon populations. These days, as a result, they are finally appreciated for their sporting qualities as well as their pulchritude.

Anglers can differentiate between Arctic and

Dolly Varden char in several ways. First, Dollies have spots that typically are smaller than the pupils of their eyes, while spots on Arctic char are generally larger than the eye pupils. Second, spawning Dolly Varden display a more pronounced hook in the lower jaw than do Arctic char; and, third, the tail of an Arctic char has a deeper fork than that of a Dolly.

Generally, spawning Arctic char take on more of a pure orange tint, while Dollies display a darker red-orange. Seen side by side, Arctic char usually have a shorter head and snout than Dollies. These differences are slight, however, and most anglers simply refer to both species as char.

Dollies or Arctic char, this bunch of anglers didn't really care. Lots of fish were being caught and that's what interested them. They couldn't get over how abundant the fish were and how much fun they were to catch.

"Just look," Ruth said, "Right this minute, every single one of the five of us has a fish on, and they're all char. Isn't it great to think of how many there must be in this river?"

REACTING TO THE TAKE

We'd headed west that morning from the airport in Anchorage and now were camped out several hundred miles away on one of Alaska's prolific wilderness rivers, the Aniak. Our outfitter, Hook-M-Up Fishing Adventures, met us at the airport in the village of Aniak, loaded us and our gear into two jet boats, and moved us more than

▲▲ *Heading down the hill to the boats for the day's fishing.*
▲ *Silver on an egg-sucking leech.*

thirty miles upriver to the waiting tent camp that would be our headquarters for the next four days.

It hadn't taken long to settle in, and now we were happily wading down river from the tents while our outfitters, Woody and Art, made dinner. Armed with Polaroid sun glasses, we easily picked out the dark red bodies of spawning sockeye salmon slowly finning at a spot where the bottom sloped off into deeper water. It was a good sign.

We weren't particularly interested in the salmon because they weren't fresh, but, since several other species invariably hang around the salmon waiting to gobble up the errant eggs, we knew there were lots of fish around to be caught.

Sure enough, we weren't disappointed. Several rainbows and Arctic grayling already had been foolish enough to mistake our egg imitations for the real thing. Now that Carolyn's char had piqued everyone's interest, that was what they specifically wanted to fish for.

"So, what were you doing that you caught a char, Carolyn? Should we be fishing differently for char than for rainbows? How do we know when we've got a char? Can you tell? Do we play it the same as the other fish?" Question after question fueled the fishing discussions.

"I do remember thinking that the fish hadn't hit the fly very hard," Carolyn reported, "but maybe it was just that it didn't leap out of the water and tear downstream like the rainbows usually do. It fought hard, but all underwater. Because he didn't jump, I didn't know he wasn't a rainbow

▲▲ *Hook-M-Up's boats transport us to all the right spots.*
▲ *A gorgeous char in the crystal-clear water of the Aniak.*

until I landed him. I really don't think I was fishing in any special way."

"No, you probably weren't," I replied. "No matter what you're fishing for, you pretty much fish an egg imitation the same way. Salmon don't build their nests in fast water. That's the way mother nature makes sure that most of the eggs will stay put in the redd. Eggs that do float out of the nest seem to tumble along, and they're usually right on the bottom where the current is the slowest. Loose eggs mean lunch for other fish, so your flies need to move like the real thing."

Hearing this, they became more careful to just let the flies dead-drift with the current. Naturally drifting flies quickly meant more frequent hookups. Then the questions about how to play the fish surfaced again. "I know I need to let a fish run or he'll break me off, but, other than that, do I play a rainbow and a char differently?" Robin asked.

"One of the main differences between rainbow and char fishing is what happens immediately after the fish takes the fly." I said. "Both species tend to take an egg fly quite delicately. Within a split second, though, the rainbow usually takes off so fast you'll feel as if he's going to pull the rod right out of your hand. He's often jumping along the way, too. The char, on the other hand, will run with the fly, but not as instantaneously nor as far. He seldom jumps. Instead, a char will move out into the current and hunker down for the fight. The antics of the rainbow may seem more desirable to some anglers, but, pound for pound, the char will give you just as good a fight."

"So, we can determine which kind of fish we have based on what he does after he takes the fly, and we have to be alert for how we react," Robin responded. "Give us some tips on playing it."

Robin was an experienced angler, too, having trout-fished in Montana and Idaho. Even though this was her first trip to Alaska and her first encounter with char, she was intent on applying her fly-fishing skills to a new situation.

"Well, since char tend to run less and use the current against you, you'll have to keep steadier pressure on them," I told her. "Many people say their arms get more tired playing a big char than they do playing a rainbow."

"Hey, I'm ready. Let's get 'em," Beth urged. A petite woman from California, Beth was just learning to fly fish. I'd had difficulty outfitting her with waders because she was so tiny. That didn't slow her down a bit. She was ready for battle. She'd listened carefully as I explained the basic overhead cast and then held her arm while she tried it out. Already she was slinging out a surprisingly accurate fly right into the midst of the Dollies where she wanted it. To her delight, she had a fish on right away.

"Let's get him in quickly before he gets off," she said. This would be her first Dolly, and she wanted it badly.

"Take your time," I advised. "Unless you let him run, most likely he'll break your leader. Besides,

▲ *Reparing a broken leader.*
▶ *They don't have anything like this in New York.*

half the fun is in matching your wits against his. Just go ahead and play him. We'll get him in when he's ready."

"Oh, those lips, those beautiful lips," she crooned a bit later as she lifted a fat fish with brightly hued mouth and sides out of the water. "Too bad they can't really pucker up, or this one would have quite a kisser."

With her confidence building after this and each subsequent fish, Beth certainly was successful that afternoon. So was everyone else. Then it was time for dinner.

THE ANIAK RIVER

Located north and east of western Alaska's regional hub, Bethel, the Aniak River originates along the western edge of the Kuskokwim Mountains and empties into the huge Kuskokwim

▲ *A cow moose and her calf swim the mighty Kuskokwim River, Alaska's second-largest.*

River at the village of Aniak. Three main headwaters, Aniak Lake and the Kipchuk and Salmon rivers, merge about sixty miles down from the lake to form the Aniak River. From that confluence until about ten miles before it joins the Kuskokwim, the Aniak provides anglers with good camping and great fishing. Some access its challenges by raft and others use jet boat transportation as we do. Either way, it's great water.

Although the Aniak has no whitewater, its fast currents, sweepers, and snag-filled pools have caught more than one rafter unprepared. Huge log jams piled up by high water from the annual spring thaw appear in new places every year. These jumbles of spruce, birch, and alder impede easy boat navigation, but provide perfect bailiwicks for fish. Branches often are decorated with flies or lures left by unsuccessful anglers who have attempted to connect with the lunkers that rest deep in the black pools beneath these bottlenecks.

Travel down the Aniak is worth the effort to navigate it. Rewards include glimpses of a multitude of Alaska's wild creatures as well as fish. Hawks cruising overhead scouting for small rodents or a female grizzly fishing the salmon runs to feed herself and her cubs are not uncommon sights. Neither are the eagles with outstretched wings silhouetted against a bright blue sky, a weasel scurrying among the river stones on the bank, or camp robbers that use their sharp beaks to invade every possible food source left unprotected.

The same careless food handling behaviors that attract birds also can invite camp invasion by one of the area's large concentration of brown and black bears. The first rule for visitors here is to keep a clean camp to avoid getting up close and personal with one of these symbols of wild Alaska. We are always careful to cook well away from the tents, avoid particularly "smelly" food like bacon, store all food in sealed containers, and burn our garbage and trash. We prefer to see our bruins at a distance!

While wildlife viewing is exciting, it is the veritable feast of fish that attracts us to the Aniak. All five species of Pacific salmon swarm into its waters, one after the other. In typical years, their numbers suggest armies heading for battle. Accompanied by the abundant Dolly Varden char, salmon join the resident rainbow trout, Arctic

▲ *Our last night is spent at Hook-M-Up's headquarters where we rig-up on the steps of one of the cabins.*

grayling, pike, and even the migrating sheefish, to provide anglers with examples of all of Alaska's piscatorial bounty. Even though we fish for all the Aniak has to offer, it's the incredible numbers of char that often astound fly fishers.

OUR CAMP

Back in camp that first afternoon Woody and his assistant guide, Art, had used the ever-present campfire to produce one of his now-famous shish kebab dinners. Some years before, one of our groups had named these delicious treats

"boo-bobs" after learning that the main ingredient was caribou meat and not beef or moose. Keeping in that tradition, the steaming caribou stroganoff that we devoured two nights later came to be called "boo-off."

Woody is a seasoned bush resident, an organized guy who seldom forgets anything associated with the dinner-fixings, and, on top of all that, is a skilled boat driver. He knows his fish and his rivers, and he loves to share that knowledge with us. Dinner time is often story time as we sit around the campfire eating, and eating, and eating.

It's no mean feat to produce the exceptional meals that Woody is so famous for given the logistical difficulties and expense of getting supplies into rural (bush) Alaska. We have to transport everything we need with us to the camp.

Jeannie, Woody's wife, who can't always go along on the trips, is present at every meal in the form of her home-baked rolls and bread, salads from her garden, and some wonderful desserts. Fry bread, a favorite staple of bush cooking, always appears in both plain and cinnamon-sugar varieties. We certainly don't want for good food. In fact, dinner is one of the highlights of the day.

By August, when we fish the Aniak, Alaska's legendary twenty-four hours of daylight are beginning to wane. Still, there's often time for fishing after dinner.

One warm, still evening (when the bugs were

especially thick), we just couldn't resist rigging up the rods with dry flies to go after what we thought were Arctic grayling dimpling the river right in front of camp. To our surprise, though, the Dollies took our flies about as often as the grayling.

Dollies are not really noted as a dry fly fish. In fact, only once before on a different river had I ever successfully dry fly fished for them. This was obviously a special night. We'd tied on a #12 elk-hair caddis, the grayling's favorite fly, and were drifting it directly to waiting fish.

Nancy was the first to notice a Dolly grab the fly intended for the grayling. "Well, look at this," she told the others, "it's a Dolly that just took my fly. That's not supposed to happen, is it?" In preparation for this trip, Nancy had been reading about the different fish in the Aniak, and which flies they prefer. Her book had not listed dry flies among the Dolly's favorites.

"Not really," I replied, "but there are no absolutes in fishing. We're constantly surprised by what fish do. Since the Dollies are interested in surface flies tonight, let's experiment and see just which ones they'll take."

Quickly I distributed another recommended dry fly, the yellow humpy, and the group gave it a try. It worked too. Then, just for fun, we switched to an Adams dry fly and the same thing happened. Amazing.

After about an hour of this unexpected dry fly fishing, the bugs became so bothersome, even with our head nets, that everyone but Carolyn

◄ *Tea by the fire after a great "boo-bob" dinner.*

▲ *Tying your own leaders.*

retreated for a cup of tea by the fire. There, the smoke kept the bugs at bay. Carolyn, remember, had catching-up to do. Soon we all headed for the sleeping bags so we could hit the river early the next morning.

WHAT KIND OF CAST?

The next morning saw high winds and intermittent rain. We'd awakened as our tent sides poofed and billowed with the gusts. Rain splattering on the tent fly made us reluctant to get up. If you wait for the rain to stop in Alaska, though, you'll stay inside forever. Besides, the fish were waiting for our flies, we could smell the coffee brewing, and nature was calling. It was time to get moving.

On our wilderness trips we often feel as though we live in our waders. If it's raining when we go to bed, we pull the waders down far enough to seat our rear ends inside the tent. The boots stay outside because it doesn't matter if they get wet. Then we scoot backwards into the tent while simultaneously peeling the waders off our legs. It's a show worthy of Funniest Home Videos. The inside-out waders then spend the night in the tent with us to stay dry and ready for the morning.

Donning our waders as best we could in the confines of a tent, we stuck our feet outside the door this particular morning to pull on our sandy wading boots. Once the gritty shoe laces were tied, we emerged into what really wasn't such a bad

"Look, there on the right," Woody cried, as we rounded a bend in the river and he quickly cut the motor. Standing at the edge of the trees was a large cow moose contentedly suckling her calf. With their huge ears alert, both looked our way. They quickly took off up the bank as they heard the commotion, but not before we got a good glimpse of the bulb-nosed mother and the adorable, big-eyed calf. What a treat.

"We'll do our best to put you on the side of the river where the wind will be behind you to help your casting," Woody told us. That side mostly put us with our backs to the bushes, however. When we moved to the more open, treeless gravel bars, the flat, unobstructed area still made things difficult.

"I can't cast," Robin wailed almost as soon as we'd hit the river. "The wind's blowing the line and fly sideways or right back at me. I need help."

Robin wasn't the only one having trouble casting in the wind. The gusts seemed to keep changing direction, making for a challenging fishing situation. We needed to try some casting alternatives to the basic overhead or roll cast, so I said, "Let's spend a few minutes on the side arm cast and the flip cast."

The side arm cast simply involves turning the overhead cast on its side. You imagine the eleven o'clock and one o'clock "stop" positions laid out on the ground, and you look down at them. The rod tip is pointing out to the side rather than up. You're also looking straight down at the face of

morning after all. The guys always rig a cover over our eating area, so we sipped our coffee and devoured the steaming egg-sausage-veggie casserole safely protected from the rain. Who could complain?

After breakfast the guides revved up the boat motors, and we took off, well protected in red, blue, and green Gore-Tex.

▲ *Just draw your rod tip back and the line will bring the fish right to you.*

your reel. After aiming your non-dominant shoulder toward the water, you cast as you would in the overhead position, within the same casting range and using the same stops and the same straight wrist. Because the fly is flipped sideways, it typically lands on the water with a ker-plunk instead of dropping to the water as happens with the overhead cast. Line mending is required right away.

"The advantage of the side arm cast is that it keeps the line close to the water where the impact of the wind is less pronounced," I told the group. "You can also side arm cast from the opposite side of your body, when conditions demand it. Just turn your body so your dominant shoulder is facing the water this time. Then, bring your arm and your rod hand across your chest, turn your reel over so that you're looking down at its backside, and cast. I held Ruth's rod hand and demonstrated.

"That's helpful," Robin said. "At least I can get my line out now," she called, as she executed a perfect side arm cast after just a couple of tries.

"If I stand over there where I want to cast, then my fly is in the bushes on my back cast whether I use either the side arm or the overhead cast," Beth complained after awhile. "Show us that flip cast you were talking about. Will that help?"

"It'll help a lot." I replied. "You generally can't get as much line out, flipping, but at least you're not in the bushes. The flip cast is more like the roll cast. With the flip, point the tip of your rod out

▲ *A nice Arctic grayling caught with a side-arm cast.*

beside you instead of up like you do in the overhead cast. Then, just flip the rod tip over quickly in a half-circle and stop it when it points straight out at the water. The line will follow the rod tip, and your fly will plop into the water. Try it."

Beth took a shot at flipping. "Look what happened," she said. "My fly landed way over on the opposite bank and not out in the water where I wanted it. What am I doing wrong?"

"You're just flipping with a little too much force," I observed. "When you have split shot on your leader, that effect is exaggerated. So, to control your flip, make sure you stop the rod when you've completed your half-circle. Remember, you're not throwing, just flipping."

A few try-out casts helped Beth put her fly where she wanted it. "I'm doing better with this cast," she decided, "and here's another fish." She crowed as the tip of her five-weight rod dipped sharply. "I guess the wind doesn't bother the fish any. This one took my fly quite greedily and now she's just trying to hide out among the salmon."

While fighting the hook, this char had, unfortunately, ended up right in the middle of the spawning beds. After a sharp nip to her back by a sockeye, she retreated downstream before Beth brought her to the bank, colorful spots and all.

This time, the fish's spots were more orange than pink, however, and her belly had turned the same color. "This fish is taking on her spawning colors," I said. "Notice that her fins have a white band along the edges.

Dollies. "You told me about the char, but I had no idea they would look like this," she said. "They are so incredibly beautiful, I'm glad I came to the Aniak and had the chance to see them. It's going to be hard to say that my favorite fish are rainbows after this."

EQUIPMENT FOR CHAR FISHING

We take 8-weight rods with us on the Aniak because we also fish for salmon there, but it is our 5-weights that get the real workout. Nine-foot rods perform best in the varied conditions on this river. With a medium-fast action, they're perfect for fish like these that frequently measure twenty inches or more.

A reel matching the rod and sporting a strong drag system is a must. Although generally we fish a weight-forward floating line in the Aniak's perfect char habitat, our reels are always outfitted with interchangeable floating and sink tip lines to enable us to get down to fish that may hold in deeper runs.

When we fish with #8 egg imitations, we use at least an 8- or 9-foot leader to help the fly drift naturally. Tippet size is usually 6-pound test, unless especially low water and spooky fish demand something smaller. Almost all egg fly fishing also requires small split shot on the leader to help keep the fly on the bottom. We carry several different sizes to accommodate different current speeds and water depths.

Besides egg flies, char will hungrily inhale a

"Both the males and females 'color up' like this as they near spawning time. They just get more and more dazzling as time goes by."

"You're right, they do," said Ruth, catching char after colorful char. "Each one is just a little bit different, but they're all breathtaking." She'd come to the Aniak to target the large rainbow trout that inhabit its waters, but, like the others, was finding that she couldn't get enough of these lustrous

▲ *A five-weight rod for the char and three eight-weight rods for salmon.*

number of other patterns, generally in size 6 or 8. Some of our favorites are a bright orange and white Frank's fly, the standby egg-sucking leech, and a muddler.

WHOOPEE

Carolyn was using the reliable flip cast and an egg-sucking leech in a steady rain as she proceeded to hook up with a fish the likes of which we hadn't seen until then.

"A salmon would take my egg-sucking leech wouldn't it?" she suddenly asked. "Whatever I have on my line is very large. If it's a salmon I don't want to break my rod."

Because the rain had clouded the water, it was hard to see what she had hooked up. I advised her to take her time, to play the fish carefully and to try bringing it close enough to the bank for us to tell whether it was one of the large scarlet-bodied sockeye we were trying to avoid.

Sockeye become very aggressive to a fly during spawning and often take flies meant for other species.

Carolyn's fish was not a salmon, though. It was a monstrous char. Her rod was bent so much I, too, was beginning to worry that it would break. The fish exerted a steady pull against her, moving closer just temporarily and then pulling away from the bank again and again. "How can you be sure he's not a salmon?" she asked.

"If it was a sockeye, he'd be red, his head would be green, he'd have a hump on his back and

▲▲ *Fishin' pals all hooked up.*
▲ *Oh, you beautiful silver.*

a huge hooked jaw. This fellow has a beautifully proportioned body and the characteristic spots. Nope, this is one large char."

The contest seemed to go on forever. It was as though Carolyn's fly was snagged on some giant log lying on the bottom. Carolyn's 5-weight rod was just barely a match for the strength and girth of this fish, but she persisted with admirable patience. Because of her restraint, he eventually tired and turned on his side, the universal sign of a tuckered-out fish.

"Wow," she exclaimed, kneeling at the edge of the river to tail him gently in preparation for release, "look at this color. His spots and belly and even his lips aren't just pink, they're a brilliant burnt orange." He was a handsome devil, indeed, the quintessence of spawning male char.

Once again, everyone gathered around to admire this specimen. At twenty-six inches long he was breathtaking. His silvery body had taken on a dark, forest green hue, and his vibrant russet spots stood out against it like neon lights. His black fins were tipped with wide white borders, and his mouth must have looked very kissable indeed to others of his kind.

"This must be a dream," Ruth said as we stood watching the incredible prize that Carolyn was reviving carefully in the shallows. "The rain has stopped, and there's a rainbow right above us."

And, so there was. From where we stood, it appeared to descend directly into the Aniak River. We'd truly found a pot of gold.

Twenty of Alaska's Best Flies

AND HOW TO TIE THEM

1. EGG-SUCKING LEECH:
(PURPLE OR BLACK)

Hook: Mustad 36890
(size #6-#2)
Weight: .25 or .30 wrapped onto the hook shank
Tail: fluffy maribou with several strands of rainbow crystal flash
Hackle: webby saddle hackle feather
Body: medium chenille, purple or black
Head: medium chenille, salmon color

Weight the hook. Tie in a fluffy maribou tail about half the length of the shank of the hook. Tie in the crystal flash.

Prepare the hackle feather and tie in by the tip with the right side of the feather facing the tyer.

Tie in the chenille for the body. Wrap the chenille forward to the bend-back of the hook and tie off. Palmer the hackle feather up to the bend-back of the hook and tie off.

Add the egg by wrapping the salmon color chenille to form an egg at the head of the fly. Tie off and whip finish.

NOTE: *The egg-sucking leech is known as the "all-Alaskan fly" because it catches virtually every species in Alaska. The most popular color combination is a purple body and salmon-colored egg-head.*

2. WOOLLY BUGGER
(PURPLE, BLACK, WHITE)

Hook: Mustad 36890 (#6-#2)
Weight: .25 or .30 wrapped onto the hook shank
Tail: fluffy maribou with several strands of rainbow crystal flash
Hackle: webby saddle hackle feather
Body: medium chenille purple, black, white, etc.

Weight the hook. Tie in a fluffy maribou tail about half the length of the shank of the hook. Tie in the crystal flash.

Prepare the hackle feather and tie in by the tip with the right side of the feather facing the tyer.

Tie in the chenille for the body. Wrap the chenille forward to the bend-back of the hook and tie off. Palmer the hackle feather up to the bend-back of the hook eye and tie off.

NOTE: *This is one of the world's best-known flies, effective in various colors for all salmon, rainbow trout, Dolly Varden char, pike, and sheefish.*

3. FISH CANDY

Hook: Mustad 7970 (#6-#2)
Weight: both weighted and un-weighted versions fish well
Body: any bright color medium or large cactus chenille

Weight the middle two thirds of the hook with lead (.25 or .30)

Wrap the chenille in tight, close wraps along the hook. (I prefer the large chenille as it makes a more dense fly.) Be careful to stroke back the fibers before each wrap to avoid flattening down the fibers of the previous wrap.

NOTE: *An easy addition is a short tail and wing of crystal flash. You can add the same or contrasting color maribou tail and wing, a bead, cone or eyeballs, saddle hackle as a collar or a strip of bunny fur as a matuka-style wing. Experiment!*

All salmon species take fish candy. Water clarity and light refraction at different times of the day may make one or the other color more effective.

4. THE COMET

Hook: Mustad 36890 (#8-#2)
Tail: a few strands of bucktail or hackle fibers
Body: flat silver tinsel or gold diamond braid
Collar: webby saddle hackle in color to match the tail
Eyes: bead chain in proportion to the hook

Tie in the eyeballs. Lay down a thread base and position the eyes on the hook. Holding the eyeball farthest away from you in your fingernails, wrap over the eyeball closest to you and under the hook several times, binding down that eyeball. Then, hold the eyeball closest to you in your fingernails and wrap over the eyeball farthest away from you and the hook several times. Once the eyeballs are secured, make figure-eight wraps over one eyeball and under the hook and then over the other eyeball and under the hook. Intersperse the figure-eights with several wraps over each individual eyeball until the eyeballs do not slide around on the hook.

Tie in the tail making it no longer than half the length of the hook shank.

Tie in the tinsel or diamond braid in front of the tail and wrap the thread forward. Now wrap the tinsel/diamond braid tightly up to the eyes.

Locate the fibers at the back end of the hackle feather (just ahead of the fluff at the base) that are about two-thirds the length of the shank of the hook. Peel off the fluff from that point down to the base of the feather leaving a bare stem. Tie in at the stem with the right side of the feather toward the tyer. Make three wraps of the feather just behind the eyes, being careful not to let it twist. Lick your fingers and stroke back the fibers of the first wrap before making the second and third wraps so the fibers sweep back along the hook. Tie off and whip finish behind the eyes.

NOTE: *The comet is a favorite Alaska pattern for sockeye salmon tied sparse and on hooks no larger than #4. It is also effective for coho salmon when tied on a #2 or 4 hook with a fuscia tail, yarn body, and collar.*

5. THE FLASH FLY

Hook: Mustad 34007 (#2)
Tail: silver flashabou
Body: silver diamond braid (weighted)
Underwing: red or orange bucktail
Wing: silver flashabou
Hackle Collar: webby red saddle hackle
Eyeballs: dumbell for weight

Tie on the eyeballs (directions with The Comet) and weight the hook.

Tie in a clump of flashabou for the tail half the length of the hook shank.

Tie in diamond braid and move the thread forward. Wrap the diamond braid to form a body to just behind the eyeballs.

Tie in a clump of bucktail that extends just to the end of the tail for the underwing, and then cover it with silver flashabou of the same length.

Remove the fluff at the base of the hackle feather. Tie in the feather by the butt, right side facing the tyer. Make three or four wraps of hackle right behind the eyes. Stroke back the fibers of each wrap and hold them in place before making the next wrap.

Whip finish behind the eyes.

NOTE: *Flash flies are an Alaska standard for silver (coho) salmon.*

Try different color combinations such as purple and chartreuse, gold and orange, etc. for times when the water is low and clear.

6. THE SOCKEYE ORANGE

Hook: Mustad 36890 (#4-#8)
Body: flat silver tinsel or diamond braid
Hackle Collar: webby orange hackle feather
Wing: black squirrel or calf tail

Attach the tinsel or diamond braid and move the thread forward. Now wrap the tinsel/diamond braid forward almost to the eye of the hook.

Discard the hackle feather fluff, then wrap it in by the butt with the right side racing the tyer. (Fibers should be no longer than the hook shank.)

Make three wraps with the feather to create the collar, being careful to stroke back the fibers before both the second and third wraps.

Stack the squirrel or calf tail and tie it in just the length of the shank. Make three thread wraps tight underneath the wing to help it stand up.

NOTE: *A sparse fly, the sockeye orange is one of Alaskans' favorites for sockeye and silver salmon. For variety, substitute green, purple, etc. for orange.*

7. THUNDER CREEK SMOLT

Hook: Tiemco 9394 (#8-#10)
Thread: white and red
Body: brown bucktail on top and white bucktail on the underside

Attach white thread to the hook about ⅔ of the way down the shank toward the eye.

Tie in a sparse clump of brown bucktail on top of the shank with the tips sticking out the front of the hook about one shank-length beyond the hook-eye.

Tie in a sparse clump of white bucktail on the underside of the shank with the tips sticking out the front of the hook the same distance as the brown bucktail.

Wrap the white thread over both clumps of bucktail down toward the eye of the hook then back to the original tie-in spot. Tie off the thread.

Attach the red thread right over the original tie-in spot.

Fold the white bucktail back along the hook and tie it down at the original tie-in spot.

Fold the brown bucktail back along the hook and tie it down in exactly the same spot.

Paste-on eyes and epoxy head are optional.

NOTE: *This is a great pattern to imitate salmon smolt, a major food source for rainbows, char and Arctic grayling in the spring when smolt are out-migrating to the sea. Fish it dead-drift on a long leader.*

8. THE BATTLE CREEK SPECIAL

Hook: Mustad 36890 (#2-#6)
Weight: .25 or .30 wrapped onto the hook shank
Thread: white or red
Tail: white maribou no longer than the shank of the hook
Body: salmon-pink chenille
Hackle: webby white saddle hackle, palmered
Collar: webby orange hackle tied at the hook eye

Weight the hook and tie in the tail.

Strip fibers from the maribou feather and stack them to make a fluffy tail.

Tie in the white saddle hackle by the tip with the right side of the feather facing the tyer.

Tie in the chenille and wrap forward to just behind the hook-eye. Tie off.

Palmer the white hackle toward the hook-eye and tie off.

Strip the fuzzy fibers off the bottom of the orange hackle feather. Tie in from the butt end right at the hook-eye with the bare stem facing out the front of the hook and the right side of the feather facing the tyer. Make three or four side-by-side wraps of the feather around the front of the hook so that the fibers separate and sweep towards the bend. Tie off. The fibers should be no longer than the hook-shank. If the feathers won't lay back, put two or three thread-wraps over them as you tie off.

NOTE: *The combination of the flesh-imitating white tail and hackle, the pink egg-imitating body and the bright orange collar of this fly make it attractive to rainbows. It likely fools fish into thinking they're getting two meals in one—an egg plus some yummy rotting salmon flesh.*

9. THE BEAD HEAD LAKE LEECH:

Bead: gold or brass in proportion to the hook size
Hook: Mustad 9672 (#8-#12)
Thread: Color to match the body
Tail: tips of the marabou plume that will form the body, plus three or four strands of rainbow flashabou
Body: marabou plume wrapped around the hook (black, brown, olive, or purple)
Wing: a few strands of marabou stripped from a feather, plus three or four strands of rainbow flashabou

Pinch the barb on the hook and insert it into the small hole of the bead.

Weight the middle two-thirds of the hook with lead wraps.

Select a bushy marabou plume (not one that has predominantly separate, straight fibers) and tie in the tips as a short (about half the shank length) tail. Add three or four strands of flashabou. Don't cut off the remainder of the plume. Wrap the thread forward.

Smooth out the plume and wrap it forward around the hook up toward the eye. Tie off just behind the bead.

Strip a few strands of marabou left on the stem (or use a new feather) and tie in just behind the bead to form a sparse wing.

Add three of four strands of flashabou to the wing and tie off.

NOTE: *The lake leech fishes effectively when trolled slowly on a sink-tip line. Black, olive, and brown are the preferred colors. In the spring when the fish are in the shallows, cast it into the shore with a floating line and retrieve with short, erratic strips. Although named a lake leech, this pattern, in black, is also fished successfully for rainbows in streams and rivers.*

10. EGG SUCKING BUNNY FLY

Hook: Mustad 9672 (#6-#8)
Thread: color to match the color of the bunny material
Body: straight-cut bunny strip

Weight the middle two-thirds of the hook with lead.

Select a narrow, straight cut bunny strip. Hold up the strip and stroke the fur to determine in which direction the fur is laying.

About half the shank length of the hook up from the end of the strip, separate the fur until the skin is exposed. (Licking your fingers and pulling the fur back from the spot keeps the fur apart and out of your field of vision.)

Tie in the strip at the tail position just where the skin is exposed. (The tail will be half the length of the hook shank.)

Do as many thread wraps as necessary (all in the same spot) to keep the skin from moving around the hook.

Move the thread forward to the eye of the hook.

Wrap the bunny strip forward to the eye of the hook in tight wraps that are angled slightly so they don't overlap.

Again, lick your fingers and separate the fur until the skin is exposed. Then tie off over the skin and not the fur. Make a neat head and whip finish.

If the finished fly seems extremely thick it may not sink well. In that case, carefully trim some fur to make the fly more sparse. Do this by inserting the tip of the scissors under the fur pointing towards the eye and snip tiny bits of fur until the fly has a more slender profile.

NOTE: *The bunny bug or flesh fly is effective for trout, steelhead, salmon, and, depending on the color, even pike. Rainbows and steelhead like black to imitate leeches, and white or light ginger color where rotting salmon flesh is available. Salmon like bright*

fuscia, chartreuse, or purple. Pike take all colors usually with the fly tied with a much longer tail that also includes flashabou or crystal flash. Also add a salmon-colored chenille egg to the front for the "egg-sucking bunny" fly.

11. ELK HAIR CADDIS

Hook: Mustad 94840 (#12-#16)
Thread: tan uni-thread 6/0
Hackle: cree, ginger, furnace, or white dry fly hackle with fibers the length of the hook gape
Dubbing: tan hare's ear with antron
Wing: stiff elk or deer hair

Lay down a thread base on the hook.

Prepare the hackle feather and tie in at the tip with the right side of the feather facing the tyer.

Dub a very sparse body.

Palmer the hackle along the hook shank leaving room for the wing.

Cut a clump of elk or deer hair just barely longer than the shank of the hook. Clean out the butts and stack the hair. Position the hair just behind the hook eye and tie in using the pinch method and eight or nine additional tight wraps to prevent hair from sliding around the hook. Keep all thread-wraps exactly on top of one another.

Finish the fly underneath the butt ends before clipping the "crew-cut" head of the fly. (Insert a half-hitch tool under the material and make six or eight half-hitches or use a whip finish tool.)

NOTE: *Grayling and rainbows generally want the elk hair caddis presented "dead drift" and squarely in the feeding lane. If it is windy, skittering the fly over the surface of the water can be successful. In Alaska, the EHC is considered to be the "never leave home without it" fly for grayling.*

12. PARACHUTE ADAMS

Hook: Mustad 94840 (#12-#14)
Post: white calf tail
Tail: grizzly hackle fibers one-half the length of the hook shank
Body: grey dubbed muskrat fur
Hackle: grizzly dry-fly hackle tied in parachute style

Take a clump of white calf tail no longer than one-half the length of the hook shank and tie it in post style just back from the hook eye.

Tie in hackle fiber tail.

Dub muskrat fur sparingly onto the hook and wrap it up to the post. Make one wrap of dubbing just in front of the post.

Tie in the hackle just behind the post and make four or five wraps around the post, parachute style.

Finish the fly with six or eight half-hitches made under the wing with a half hitch tool or a whip finisher.

NOTE: *This universally popular mayfly imitation is used for rainbows and Arctic grayling all season long. The white post provides better visibility.*

13. HUMPY

Hook: Mustad 94840 (#12-#14)
Tail: deer hair
Underbody: yellow or red floss
Overbody: deer hair
Wing: tips of the deer hair used to make the body
Hackle: brown and grizzly mixed

Tie in deer hair tips about half the length of the shank for the tail.

Tie in a long clump of deer hair by the butts with the tips sticking out the back of the hook.

Tie in the yellow floss and wrap the thread forward. Then wrap the floss along three fourths of the hook shank toward the hook eye.

Fold the deer hair over the floss body and secure it about three fourths of the way down the hook shank.

Take the tips of the deer hair and make several wraps in front of the clump to help it stand up. Then do three or four figure-eight wraps around each half of the clump of tips to divide them.

Make several wraps of brown and grizzly hackle both in back and in front of the deer hair wing.

NOTE: *The humpy is another effective dry fly for Alaska's grayling and rainbows.*

14. GOLD RIBBED HARE'S EAR

Hook: Mustad 3906B (#10-#12)
Tail: guard hairs from hare's mask or several hackle fibers
Ribbing: thin gold wire
Body: dubbed hare's ear with antron (tan)
Wingcase: a section of mottled turkey feather in proportion to the hook

Weight the front one-third of the hook with lead wraps.

Tie in the guard hair or hackle fiber tail.

Tie in the gold ribbing.

Dub the thread and wrap ⅔ of the way down the hook toward the eye.

Rib over the dubbing and tie off.

Tie in the strip of turkey feather with the right side down just at the point where the dubbing stopped.

Dub the thread and wrap the remaining ⅓ of the hook making it thicker than the back to simulate the thorax of the nymph.

Fold the turkey feather strip loosely over the dubbed thorax so as not to flatten the dubbing and tie it off.

Whip finish, then carefully pick out the guard hair with a dubbing tool to imitate legs.

NOTE: *The gold-ribbed hare's ear is the one nymph that is always a good producer for rainbows and Arctic grayling. It's another "don't leave home without it" Alaska fly. Tie it in tan for rivers and in olive with a pearl flashabou wing case for lakes.*

15. PHEASANT TAIL NYMPH

Hook: Mustad 3906B (#10-#12)
Tail: the tips of three or four pheasant tail fibers
Ribbing: thin gold wire
Wingcase: pheasant tail fibers
Thorax: Peacock herl

Select several long pheasant tail fibers and tie in their tips to form the tail of the fly. Do not cut off the remainder of the fibers. The tail should be about one-half the length of the hook shank.

Tie in the ribbing just in front of the tail and wrap the thread forward.

Wrap the pheasant tail fibers into a lose rope and then wrap the rope two-thirds of the way down the hook toward the eye.

Rib over the pheasant tail wraps and tie off. Do not cut off the remainder of the pheasant fibers.

Tie in three or four peacock herl strands in front of the remaining pheasant tail fibers and wrap them around each other loosely to form a rope. Wrap the rope up toward the eye of the hook to form the thorax.

Fold the remaining pheasant tail fibers loosely over the peacock herl thorax to form the wingcase and tie off.

NOTE: *The pheasant tail is essential to have in an Alaska fly box. The mayfly hatches here are not as prolific as in the Lower 48 but our fish still feed heavily on mayfly nymphs. At those times, this fly is still one of the best.*

16. ZUG BUG NYMPH

Hook: Mustad 3906B (#10-#12)
Tail: tips of peacock herl strands
Body: peacock herl
Ribbing: fine silver or gold wire
Wingcase: mottled turkey feather strip

Select four strands of peacock herl and stack them with all the tips together.

Tie in the tips of the peacock herl to form a tail about one-half the length of the hook shank.

Tie in the silver ribbing and wrap the thread forward.

Wrap the strands of peacock herl loosely together to form a rope and then wrap the rope along the shank of the hook.

Rib the shank of the hook over the peacock herl and tie off.

Tie in the strip of turkey feather at the eye of the hook and trim to just one-third of the length of the shank.

Tie off and whip finish.

NOTE: *The zug bug is simple to tie and effective on both trout and grayling as a stonefly imitation. You'll be glad you have it along.*

17. BLACK STONEFLY NYMPH

Hook: Mustad 3906B (#10-#12)
Tail: two black goose biots
Ribbing: fine copper wire
Body: black hare's ear/antron dubbing topped by black swiss straw
Wingcase: black swiss straw
Hackle: black
Antenna: two long black goose biots

Tie in the two black goose biots to form a forked tail.

Tie in the copper wire.

Tie in a strip of black swiss straw again as long as the hook shank.

Dub the thread and then wrap two thirds of the way toward the eye of the hook.

Pull the strip of swiss straw over the top of the dubbed body.

Rib over the swiss straw and tie off but do not cut off the remaining swiss straw.

Tie in the hackle by the tip in front of the remaining swiss straw.

Dub the thorax. Then, palmer the hackle forward to the eye of the hook.

Fold the swiss straw back over a small portion of the body and hold it in place with a bodkin. Then, fold the straw back over the bodkin toward the front of the hook to form a folded wing case. Tie down and repeat the process to form a second wing case in front of the first.

Folding the swiss straw to form the wing cases flattens the hackle and forms the legs.

Trim legs as preferred, tie off, and whip finish.

NOTE: *This is a more realistic but harder-to-tie imitation of the stonefly nymph than the zug bug. A few of these should always have a spot in any nymph collection for Alaska's rivers.*

18. MUDDLER MINNOW

Hook: Mustad 9672 (#6-#10)
Tail: mottled turkey feather segment
Body: gold tinsel or diamond braid
Underwing: gray or brown squirrel tail

Overwing: twin segments of mottled turkey quill
Head: spun deer hair

Tie in the turkey segment for the tail about a third of the length of the hook.

Tie in the tinsel or diamond braid and wrap the thread forward. Now, wrap the tinsel or diamond braid forward three-quarters of the way down the hook toward the eye.

Tie in the squirrel tail underwing extending it just to the tip of the tail.

Top the underwing with matched turkey quill segments that also extend just to the tip of the tail.

Spin the deer hair to form a dense head, then trim to desired shape.

NOTE: *This classic fly has just as many admirers up north as anywhere else. Effective for rainbows and cutthroat trout, it's also taken many an Alaskan steelhead and char.*

19. GLO BUG

Hook: Mustad 92567R (#6-#12)
Thread: Uni-thread 6/0 in color to match the yarn
Body: two short strands of Glo-Bug yarn (of various colors) and one short strand of flame Glo-Bug yarn

Lay a narrow thread base down exactly in the center of the hook shank.

Sandwich the strand of flame-colored Glo-bug yarn between the other two strands and place on top of the thread base.

Make three tight thread wraps overlapping each other exactly in the center of the material and pull tight to make the yarn flare.

Hold up the yarn and make three wraps around the base of the material. Then make three turns of thread under and in front of the yarn.

Whip finish.

Hold all three strands of yarn tightly together and straight up. Cut all three at once with a very sharp scissors and then work the yarn between your fingers to fluff it and spread it underneath the hook.

Trim to shape.

NOTE: *Glo-bugs are one of the two egg imitation flies that take more rainbows and char than any other fly when salmon are spawning in Alaska. Fished dead-drift, they imitate the real salmon eggs bouncing along the bottom of the stream that provide almost pure protein in a fish's diet.*

20. ILIAMNA PINKIE

Hook: Mustad 92567R (#6-#12)
Body: salmon pink chenille

Lay down a short thread base exactly in the middle of the shank of the hook. Weight with lead wire if desired and wrap the thread forward.

Tie in chenille by its white center thread.

Depending on the hook-size, make two side-by-side wraps of chenille and one wrap over the top to form an egg shape. With larger size hooks, wrap three wraps, then two, then one to form the egg shape.

Tie off and whip finish.

NOTE: *This is the second of the two egg-imitation flies used in Alaska. Have in your fly box eggs of several different sizes and several different shades as it is often difficult to determine which of the five Pacific salmon species' eggs the rainbows may be feeding on at any given time. The Iliamna pinkie also is used extensively for Alaska's steelhead.*

▶ *Sunrise and Alaska fireweed.*

Appendices

INFORMATION & RESOURCES FOR PLANNING A TRIP TO ALASKA

LOCATIONS

BROOKS RIVER

Brooks Lodge/Katmailand
4125 Aircraft Drive
Anchorage AK 99502
(907) 243-0649
www.katmailand.com

Katmai National Park
P.O. Box 7
King Salmon, AK 99613
(907) 246-3305
www.nps.gov/katm

Alaska Department of Fish & Game
P.O. Box 37
King Salmon, AK 99613
(907) 246-3341
www.ak.gov/adfg/sportf/sf_home.htm
www.sf.adfg.state.ak.us/statewide/regu
    lations/2002/bristolbay/PDFs/02B
    BNak.pdf/

Penair
6100 Boeing Ave
Anchorage, AK 99502
(907) 243-2323
www.penair.com/

Katmai Country
Alaska Geographic Society
Volume 16, No. 1, 1989

KODIAK ISLAND

Kodiak Island Convention & Visitors
    Bureau
100 Marine Way
Kodiak, AK 99615
(907) 486-4782
www.kodiak.org

Kodiak National Wildlife Refuge
    Center
1390 Buskin Road
Kodiak, AK 99615
(907) 487-2600

Alaska Department of Fish & Game
211 Mission Road
Kodiak, Ak 99615
(907) 486-1880
www.ak.gov/adfg/sportf/sf_home.htm

Alaska Airlines
(800) 252-7422
www.alaskaair.com

ERA Aviation
(907) 248-4422
www.eraaviation.com

Kodiak
Alaska Geographic Society
Volume 19, No. 3, 1992

ANIAK RIVER

Hook-M-Up Fishing Adventures
P.O. Box 347
Aniak, AK 99557
(907) 467-6136
www.fishhookmupalaska.com

Alaska Department of Fish & Game
460 Ridgecrest Drive, Room 215
Bethel, AK 99559
(907) 543-1677
www.ak.gov/adfg/sportf/sf_home.htm

Penair
6100 Boeing Avenue
Anchorage, AK 99502
(907) 243-2323

Frontier Flying Service
5245 Airport Industrial Way
Fairbanks, AK 99709
(800) 478-6779

The Kuskokwim River
Alaska Geographic Society
Volume 15, No. 4, 1988

TALACHULITNA RIVER

Talstar Lodge
P.O. Box 870978
Wasilla, AK 99687
(907) 688-1116 (winter)
(907) 733-1672 (summer)

Alaska Department of Fish & Game
333 Raspberry Road
Anchorage, AK 99518
(907) 267-2100
www.ak.gov/adfg/sportf/sf_home.htm

Regal Air
4506 Lakeshore Dr.
Anchorage, AK 99502
(907) 243-8535

TANGLE LAKES/TANGLE RIVER

Tangle Lakes Lodge
P.O. Box 670386
Chugiak, AK 99567
(907) 688-9173
http://www.alaskan.com/tanglelakes/

Bureau of Land Management
Glennallen District Office
P.O. Box 147
Glennallen, AK 99588
(907) 822-3217
http://www.glennallen.ak.blm.gov

Alaska Department of Fish & Game
P.O. Box 47
Glennallen, AK 99588
www.ak.gov/adfg/sportf/sf_home.htm

Paxson Lodge
Paxson, AK 99737
(907) 822-3330

INFORMATION & RESOURCES FOR PLANNING A TRIP TO ALASKA

FLOAT TUBING

ANCHORAGE LAKES
Alaska Department of Fish & Game
333 Raspberry Road
Anchorage, AK 99518
(907) 267-2100
www.ak.gov/adfg/sportf/sf_home.htm

PALMER-MATANUSKA VALLEY LAKES
Alaska Department of Fish & Game
1800 Glenn Highway, Suite 4
Palmer, AK 99761
(907) 746-6300
www.ak.gov/adfg/sportf/sf_home.htm

FLY-IN FLOAT TUBING

Scenic Mountain Air
P.O. Box 4
Moose Pass, AK 99631
(907) 288-3646

CANOE RENTAL

Talkeetna Camp & Canoe
P.O. Box 378
Talkeetna, AK 99676
(907) 733-2732

Tippecanoe
P.O. Box 1175
Willow, AK 99688
(907) 495-6688

OTHER WEB SITES

Anchorage Convention & Visitors
   Bureau
www.anchorage.net

Alaska Visitors Association
www.visitalaska.org

Alaska Division of Tourism
www.dced.state.ak.us/tourism

Alaska State Parks (public cabin
   rental)
www.dnr.state.ak.us/parks/parks.htm

Alaska Marine Highway System
www.dot.state.ak.us/

Alaska Department of Fish & Game
www.ak.gov/adfg/sportf/sf_home.htm

Alaska's National Parks
www.nps.gov/akso/gis/akparks.htm

Reserve a National Forest Service
   Cabin
www.reserveusa.com

Alaska Book Adventures
www.epicenterpress.com

OTHER BOOKS

*Fishing Alaska on Dollars a Day, 3rd
   Edition,* Christopher & Adela
   Batin, 1995, Alaska Angler
   Publications, Fairbanks, Alaska

*How To Rent A Public Cabin In South
   Central Alaska,* Andromeda
   Romano-Lax, 1999, Wilderness
   Press, Berkeley, California

*The Milepost, All The North Travel
   Guide,* 55th Edition, Kris Valencia
   Graef, Editor, 2003, Morris
   Communications, Augusta,
   Georgia

RECOMMENDED EQUIPMENT & GEAR FOR ALASKA FLY FISHING

RODS

Salmon

9 foot, 8 weight for sockeye, pink, chum, and silver salmon

9 foot, 8 weight for steelhead, pike & sheefish

9 foot, 10 weight for king salmon

Salmon rods should have a medium-fast action (flex) with a strong butt section for maintaining leverage against a large fish

Trout

9 foot, 5 weight for rainbows, Dolly Varden char, and Arctic grayling

Medium action (flex) rods are recommended for all but the largest trout and char

Rods should be protected by cloth sleeves and transported in metal tubes or PVC pipe. Bring at least one spare rod (9 foot, 8 weight is recommended). It is not always possible to get a rod repaired quickly in Alaska.

REELS

Reels should be designed to hold a line-weight to match the rod and be equipped with a very strong drag system. Maintenance-free reels with easily interchangeable spools are recommended. Since much of Alaska's water is brackish, it is also wise to bring reels that are anodized to protect against corrosion from salt water. Bring at least one spare reel to match each rod weight. It is not always possible to get a reel repaired quickly in Alaska.

LINES

Line weights should match each rod. Reels should be equipped with both weight-forward floating and sink-tip lines for variable fishing conditions. Except for float tubing, fifteen-foot intermediate sink tip lines will suffice for most fishing situations. Fast sink tip lines may be recommended by specific locations. Inquire of the outfitter or lodge prior to the trip.

LEADERS

Leader type/size to match the target species is required. Inquire of outfitter or lodge prior to the trip. Generally, leaders that taper to fifteen-twenty-five pound tippet are required for all but the largest king salmon fishing. Other salmon fishing requires tippets of twelve-fifteen pound test. Most rainbow and char fishing requires leaders tapering to tippets of six-eight pound test. Arctic grayling fishing requires tippets of four-six pound test. If traveling into rural Alaska, bring plenty of leader material and, if building your own leader, bring a couple of extra knot-tyers.

SPLIT SHOT

Bring a split-shot dispenser with several different sizes of shot. A split-shot or two are often used on a leader to get a fly to the bottom, even if the fly fisher is using a sink-tip line.

WADING STAFF

The use of a wading staff for safety is advisable on many Alaska rivers. Recommended: A collapsible, medium-weight (or thicker), shock-corded staff that can be carried in a belt pouch.

VEST/CHEST-PACK/FANNY-PACK

Personal preference should guide you. Be sure it contains a needle-nosed pliers, a couple of hook sharpeners, dry-fly floatant, etc. Many people also bring a good waterproof day pack for use on the boat/airplane.

RAIN GEAR

Fishers are advised to bring top-quality rain jackets and pants. Knee-high rubber boots are recommended.

WADERS

Both neoprene and breathable waders are used in Alaska. If the water you will be fishing is glacial, neoprene waders are recommended. Many visitors bring a pair of both types of waders for different conditions. In that case, stocking foot waders are advisable so only one pair of wading boots is necessary. Always bring an extra pair of shoelaces.

OTHER

Layered clothing will enable the fly fisher to add or remove pieces of clothing to match weather conditions. Cold, rainy weather is common in Alaska in the summer time. Don't be caught without warm clothes! Don't wear jeans under your waders. Bring light-weight fleece pants or expedition-weight long janes to wear instead. Good Polaroid sunglasses are a must. Bring a spare pair. A wool hat and fingerless gloves also should be in your pack as should a head-net for mosquitoes. Always bring a spare baseball cap as well.

FLY FISHING CLUBS FOR WOMEN

February 1, 2003

UNITED STATES

ARIZONA

Dame Juliana Anglers
600 W. Ray Rd., Suite B-6
Chandler, AZ 85225-3908
damejuliana@yahoo.com
www.devpros.com/dja/

CALIFORNIA

Golden West Women Flyfishers
790 27th Ave.
San Francisco, CA 94121
krieger@aimnet.com
www.gwwf.org

The Irresistibles
2042 Alexander Dr.
Escondido, CA 92025

The Ladybugs Fly Fishing Club
3340 Lariat Dr.
Cameron, CA 95682
fishen@directcon.net
www.theladybugs.com

Shasta Mayflies
PO Box 992776
Redding, CA 96099-2776
fishladyfromca@webtv.net

COLORADO

Colorado Women Flyfishers
PO Box 101137
Denver, CO 80250
info@colowomenflyfishers.org
www.colowomenflyfishers.org

CONNECTICUT

Connecticut Women Anglers on the Fly
24 Dryden Dr.
Meriden, CT 06450
frostydcs@aol.com

DELAWARE

Delaware Valley Women's Fly Fishing
    Association
25 Marple Rd.
Haverford, PA 19041
info@dvwffa.org
www.dvwffa.org

FLORIDA

Emerald Coast Fly Rodders
PO Box 1131
Fort Walton Beach, FL 32549
fishnlady1@aol.com

GEORGIA

Georgia Women Flyfishers
119 South McDonough St.
Decatur, GA 30030
gawomfly@bigfoot.com
www.georgiaflyfishing.com

ILLINOIS

Chicago Women's Casting & Angling
    Club
1400 N. State Parkway, No. 8
Chicago, IL 60610
chicagoanglingandcastingclub@yahoo.
    com

MAINE

Tacky Women's Angler Team
PO Box 1
Anson, ME 04911
trueview@somtel.com

MARYLAND

Chesapeake Women Anglers
612 - 39th Ave.
Hyattsville, MD 20782
njkawecki@juno.com
www.chesapeakewomenanglers.org

MICHIGAN

Flygirls
PO Box 828
Pentwater, MI 49449
annrmiller@aol.com
www.flygirls.ws

MINNESOTA

Wading Women of Minnesota
PO Box 11383
St. Paul, MN 55111-0383
wadingwomen@hotmail.com

Women Anglers of Minnesota
PO Box 580653
Minneapolis, MN 55468

MONTANA

Gallatin Valley Wad'n Women
316 S. Lindley Place, No. 5
Bozeman, MT 59715
gvwwbozeman@yahoo.com

NEW JERSEY

Delaware Valley Women's Fly Fishing
    Association
25 Marple Rd.
Haverford, PA 19041
info@dvwffa.org
www.dvwffa.org

FLY FISHING CLUBS FOR WOMEN

Joan Wulff Fly Fishers
PO Box 1782
Passaic, NJ 07055
joanwulfflyfishers@yahoo.com

NEW MEXICO

She Fishes!
2820 Richmond Ave. NE
Albuquerque, NM 87107
shadowbot@aol.com
www.homestead.com/shefishesnm

NEW YORK

The Dame Anglers
5 Lower Rd.
Westtown, NY 10998
dameang@warwick.net

Julianna Anglers
FDR Station
PO Box 7220
New York, NY 10150
hoopsnflies@msn.com
www.julianasanglers.com

Ladies in Wading
108 Drake Rd.
Lansing, NY 14882
loveflyfishing@gateway.net

NORTH CAROLINA

Women on the Fly
4732 Sharon Rd.
Charlotte, NC 28210
Womenonfly@aol.com

OREGON

Damsel Flies
PO Box 3932
Eugene, OR 97402
Oregondamselflies@hotmail.com

The Lady Anglers Fishing Society
17084 S. Monroe
Mulino, OR 97042

PENNSYLVANIA

Delaware Valley Women's Fly Fishing
    Association
25 Marple Rd.
Haverford, PA 19041
info@dvwffa.org
www.dvwffa.org

RHODE ISLAND

Ladies of the Long Rod
203 Sterling Ave.
Providence, RI 02909
awriter203@earthlink.net

SOUTH CAROLINA

Women in Waders
3 Cateswood Dr.
Spartanburg, SC 29302
armstrongellen@msn.com

TENNESSEE

Tennessee Brookies
6510 Westland Dr.
Knoxville, TN 37919
tnbrookies@aol.com

TEXAS

Texas Women Fly Fishers
7310 S. Congress, No. 106
Austin, TX 78745
cwhiston@io.com
www.twff.net

UTAH

Damselfly
appleday@airswitch.net

VIRGINIA

Reel Ladies
2756 Avenel Ave. SW
Roanoke, VA 24015
reellady@mindspring.com

Lady Highlanders
16501 Jeb Stuart Hwy.
Abingdon, VA 24211
dcrabtree@cablenet-va.com
www.ladyhighlanders.org

WASHINGTON

Northwest Women Flyfishers
PO Box 31020
Seattle, WA 98103
nwflyfishers@hotmail.com
www.northwestwomenflyfishers.org

Southwest Washington Lady Flyfishers
110 Penny Lane
Kelso, WA 98626
fishnchicks@earthlink.net
www.fishnchicks.org

WISCONSIN

Wisconsin Sportswomen Club
W237 N. 1480 Busse Rd.
Waukesha, WI 53188

Glossary

Action—The degree of flexibility in a fly rod. Fast-action rods flex only near the tip of the rod, medium-action rods flex about a third of the way from the tip, and slow-action rods flex about halfway down from the rod tip. (*See Flex.*)

Anadromous—Fish species that are born in fresh water, migrate to the ocean and live part of their lives there, and subsequently return to fresh water to spawn and die. Salmon, steelhead trout, and char are examples of anadromous species.

Arctic grayling—A member of the salmonid family generally found in only the purest water. It is characterized by its huge, sail-like dorsal fin.

Backcast—When the line rolls out behind the caster during false casting.

Backing—Narrow, braided line that attaches the fly line to the reel. Used to help fill up the spool and allow fish to make runs longer than the fly line.

Barb—The upward slanted bit of metal immediately behind the point of the hook. Flattening the barb with needle nosed pliers forms a barbless hook.

Bead head—A fly with a metal or glass bead inserted on the hook to just behind the hook eye.

Blood knot—A knot with which two or more segments of monofilament line, not too disparate in diameter, are connected to form a leader. Also known as the barrel knot.

Bucktail—Hair from a deer's tail used in the wings and tails of many flies.

Butt—The section of the fly rod containing the cork handle that the angler holds or the rear section of the leader that is connected to the fly line.

Caddis fly—A prolific moth-like insect that is one of the most important foods for fish.

Cast—The act of moving the fly rod backwards and forwards in order to send the line out onto the water; also, a leader that has two or more flies attached.

Channel—A slot formed by the current that directs water along a certain path.

Char—A species of fish related to trout. Alaska has Dolly Varden and Arctic char.

Chum—A species of Pacific salmon. Males develop red stripes along their sides when spawning. Also referred to as "dog" salmon.

Current—Water flow caused by gravity or tides.

Dead drift—A technique that enables the fly to float downstream freely with the current, unimpeded by line or leader, in imitation of natural insects.

Downstream—The direction in which river water is flowing away from the angler.

Drag—When water currents, wind, or the leader cause the fly to drift in a manner different from the way a real insect or baitfish would drift or behave. Drag also refers to the braking device in a fishing reel.

Drift—To be transported or moved from one location to another by action of the water.

Dry/dry fly—A type of fly designed to imitate a winged insect floating on the water.

Emerger—An insect during the time when it is moving to the surface of the water and preparing to hatch into a winged adult.

False cast—A forward and backward motion of the rod and line in the air that allows the angler to get sufficient line out to make the cast or to dry the fly.

Feeding lane—A narrow line of the current that carries food to a fish.

Glossary

Feeding lie—The location where a fish waits for food to drift by.

Flex—Refers both to the degree of bend in a fly rod and to the location of the bend. Full-flex rods bend along almost their entire length. Tip-flex rods bend only at the tip of the rod and mid-flex rods bend about halfway down from the rod tip. Mid-flex rods are the easiest to cast over long periods of time. *(See Action.)*

Floatant—Substances that add flotation or buoyancy to dry flies.

Floating—A type of fly line that is constructed so that it remains on the water's surface

Fly rod—A particular type of rod that casts a fly line. Usually made of graphite, it is typically longer and more tapered than other types of fishing rods.

Float tube—A floating device in which the angler sits and paddles around a lake or pond; also known as a "belly boat."

Fly line—A type of fishing line designed to be cast by a fly rod. It is comprised of a core and a coating that can be modified to meet specific fishing needs.

Fry—The fish just after it has hatched from the egg.

Gape—On a fly hook, the width between the hook shank and the point that determines hook size (sometimes referred to as the gap.)

Graphite—Material used in the construction of strong, flexible and light-weight fly rods.

Guide—The metal or ceramic loops set out along a fly rod through which the line passes as it is cast. Also one who assists another to fish.

Hackle—Feathers from a chicken or game bird's neck or back that are used in making fishing flies.

Handle—The cork grip the angler holds when casting. Also, the piece of metal that turns the spool on the fly reel.

Hatch—The time when large numbers of insects break out onto the surface of the water or nearby vegetation and become airborne.

Haul—A swift, short pull on the fly line to achieve more casting distance and speed. Called the double haul when done on both the forward and back cast.

Hold—A place in a river or stream where fish can rest or wait for the current to deliver food. Often located behind an obstruction or along undercut banks or banks with slow, deep current.

Hook eye—The small ring or loop at the front of the hook to which the leader can be attached.

Hook shank—The long part of the hook between the hook eye and the place where the hook bends.

Hook size—The identification number of a hook that is determined by the width of the hook gape between the point and the shank, not the length of the shank. The larger the number, the smaller the hook (e.g. #24 is a very small hook; #4 is a large one).

Improved clinch knot—The knot most frequently used to tie the fly onto the leader when fishing clinch knot for large fish.

Indicator—A floating device (plastic beads, small balls of yarn, a short piece of fly line, etc.) that is attached to the leader to tell the angler when a fish has taken the fly. Usually called "strike indicators."

Landing—Bringing a fish to the shore or to the boat to keep or to release.

Leader—The length of monofilament extending from the fly line to the fly. It can be a knotless leader made from a single strand of material or one in which several pieces of monofilament of decreasing diameter are connected by knots such as the blood or triple surgeon's knot.

Leech—An aquatic worm found in streams and lakes often referred to as a bloodsucker. The leech is a favorite food of fish. Also refers to a fly that imitates a leech.

Line hand—The hand that holds the line while the fly angler casts or strips in line while fishing.

Line weight—The diameter and strength of a fly line related to what size of fish it will catch and what size of rod should cast it. Line weight and rod weight must match for the rod to cast properly.

Load/loading—When the weight of the fly line bends the rod tip during the cast in order to send the line out.

Mayflies—Aquatic insects that are a favorite food of fish. The adults have upswept wings, bodies, and tails.

Mending—Using the rod tip to move the fly line and leader into a different position, either in the air or on the water, to enable the fly to float freely. Usually achieved with an upstream flip of the rod tip.

Milt—The male fish's reproductive secretions.

Monofilament—Nylon fishing line used for making leaders or wound onto spinning reels.

Nail knot—The knot used to connect the butt of the leader to the fly line.

Nippers—Clippers used to trim tag ends of various knots.

Nymph—One of the underwater life stages of an aquatic bug before it becomes an airborne adult; also, the fly that imitates those life stages.

Overhead—The movement of the fly rod and line backwards to a stop and then cast forward to a stop in preparation for delivering the fly and placing it on the water.

Palming—Pressing the palm of one hand flat up against or beneath the exposed outer rim of the reel in order to slow the run of a hooked fish.

Pickup—Lifting the fly line off the water for the first stage of the cast.

Polarization—Treatment in the manufacture of sunglasses that reduces glare to enable the angler to better see the fish.

Pool—A slow moving part of a river, usually with significant depth, whose surface is usually unbroken.

Pound test—The breaking strength of monofilament fishing line.

Presentation—Placement of the fly on the water and the way the fly is fished.

Rapids—Where the water of a river flows over large boulders with great force.

Reach cast—The movement of the rod tip upriver, to the right or left, before the line hits the water to facilitate a longer, drag-free drift of the fly.

Redd—The nest in the sand or gravel of a river which the female fish creates with her body or her tail and into which she drops her eggs.

Reel seat—The locking device at the end of the rod behind the handle that holds the reel in place.

Riffles—Where the water of a river flows over small stones or rocks and causes lots of bubbles or foam; typically these are very shallow.

Rise—When the fish comes to the surface of the water to investigate or consume an insect.

Rod hand—The hand that holds the cork handle of the fly rod while casting or fishing. *(See also Line hand.)*

Rod weight—The numerical rating of a fly rod based on the size of fish it can catch and the size of the line it will cast. Generally, 3-, 4-, 5- and 6-weight rods are used for pan

fish, trout, and bass, while 7-, 8-, 9-, and 10-weight rods are used for salmon, steelhead, pike etc. Twelve weight and higher rods are used for saltwater fishing.

Roll cast—A cast used to keep the fly out of obstructions behind the caster. Line is pulled across the water to a stop as the casting hand reaches the caster's shoulder and then is sent forward in a quick upward and flipped-over motion.

Run—A section of water in a river that typically flows more slowly and deeply than the water either directly upstream or downstream; also the action of a fish that is hooked and being played by the angler.

Salmonid—Any of a family of elongate, soft-finned fishes (like salmon and trout) that have the last vertebrae upturned.

Sink rate—How fast the tip of the fly line sinks in the water.

Sinking tip—A fly line that has a weighted portion at the tip to send and keep the fly underwater. The weighted portion may be of varying lengths, to sink more or less line, and of varying density, to affect the speed with which the line sinks.

Slack—A condition in which the line is loose and without tension. Slack line facilitates a drag-free drift of the fly, but it may cause an angler to lose a hooked fish.

Smolt—Juvenile fish that can be a major food source for larger fish

Smoltification—The physiological process in anadromous fish that permits their bodies to enter the ocean and derive oxygen from saltwater and then to reverse the process when returning to fresh water to spawn.

Spawn(ing)—Reproductive activity of fish. The female digs a nest, or redd, with her tail and deposits her eggs. The male then swims alongside her or above the eggs and releases milt to fertilize them. Also, the migration of Pacific salmon to their home streams for mating, egg fertilization, and death.

Split shot—Balls of lead of different sizes, which an angler can pinch onto the leader to make the leader and fly sink.

Streamer—A fly that imitates bait fish or leeches.

Strike—A piece of floating material tied on the leader to help the fly fisher detect the strike of a fish underwater.

Stripping (v.)—Pulling in the fly line and the fly with the line over the fingers of the rod hand and with differing types of movements.

Stripping (n.)—The metal line-guide or loop closest to the cork handle of the fly rod guide.

Stoneflies—Aquatic insects that live among the rocks of lakes and streams, migrate to shore, and metamorphose into adults. In both the nymph and adult life stages they are a significant food source for fish.

Surgeon's—A knot used to tie varying sizes of monofilament together when knot constructing leaders or tying a tippet on to a leader.

Take—When a fish gets hold of or strikes the fly or a real insect or another food source.

Tailing—Landing a fish by grasping it just in front of its tail; also a type of loop made by the line while casting.

Tailing loop—A poorly executed cast where the fly line drops below the tip of the rod during the cast. Usually results in the fly not being delivered correctly.

Tapered—A commercially made knotless leader that tapers from a large to small diameter. It has a loop on the end to permit a loop-to-loop connection.

Tide—The result of the earth's gravitational pull on water causing the periodic rise and fall of oceans and seas and affecting the speed and depth of coastal rivers.

Tippet—The portion of the leader to which the fly is tied.

Troll—To tow a fly or lure behind a moving boat or float tube.

Upstream—The direction from which water flows toward the fish and the angler.

Waders—Chest-high, waterproof protection pulled on over the angler's clothes. May be made of rubber, neoprene, or breathable materials and may include attached boots or be worn with separate boots. Not to be confused with hip boots, which come only to the angler's thigh.

Wading—Walking in the water. Also a staff used by a fly fisher to help provide stability when wading in stick/staff rivers or streams, usually collapsible and carried on a belt.

Weight-forward—A type of floating fly line in which the densest portion is toward the forward end to which the tippet and the fly are attached.

Wet fly—A fly fished under the water and used to imitate insects, leeches, small fish, crustaceans, etc.

Wind knot—A knot that forms in the leader because of incorrect casting strokes.

Bibliography

BOOKS BY WOMEN

▲ *Laurie, a flyfishing woman.*

BOOKS ON FLY FISHING

A Different Angle: Fly Fishing Stories By Women, Holly Morris, 1995, Seal Press, Seattle, Washington

A Woman's Guide To Fly Fishing Favorite Waters, Yvonne Graham, editor, 2000, David Communications, Sisters, Oregon

Cast Again, Jennifer Olsson, 1997, The Lyons Press, New York

Cathy Beck's Fly-Fishing Handbook, The Lyons press, 2002, New York

Fly Casting Accuracy, Joan Wulff, 1997, Linden Publishing, Fresno, California

Fly Casting Techniques, Joan Wulff, 1995, The Lyons Press, New York

Fly Fishing: A Woman's Guide, Dana Rikimaru, 2000, Ragged Mountain Press/McGraw-Hill, Camden, Maine

Fly Fishing: Expert Advice From a Woman's Perspective, Joan Wulff, 1991, Stackpole Books, Mechanicsburg, Pennsylvania

Little Rivers: Tales of a Woman Angler, Margo Page, 1995, Lyons Press, New York

Reel Women, Lyla Foggia, 1995, Beyond Words Publishing, Hillsboro, Oregon

Reading the Water, Mallory Burton, 1995, Keokee Co. Publishing Co., Sandpoint, Idaho

BOOKS ON ALASKA

Alaska Fishing, 2nd edition, Rene Limeres & Gunnar Pedersen, 1997, Foghorn Press, Petaluma, California

Flies For Alaska: A Guide to Buying & Tying, Anthony J. Route, 1991, Johnson Books, Boulder, Colorado

Fly Patterns of Alaska, Alaska Flyfishers, Dirk Derksen, Editor, 1993, revised edition, Frank Amato Publications, Portland, Oregon

Flyfishing Alaska, Anthony J. Route, 1995, Spring Creek Press, Estes Park, Colorado

How To Catch Alaska's Trophy Sportfish, Christopher Batin, 1984, Alaska Angler Publications, Fairbanks, Alaska

Index

About the Author and Photographer

An Alaskan since 1969, Cecilia "Pudge" Kleinkauf is an attorney and a retired university professor. For the past sixteen years, her company, Women's Flyfishing®, has taught women how to fly fish and taken them on guided trips throughout Alaska to find the best fishing for salmon, trout, char, Arctic grayling, and other species. Off-season, she leads saltwater fly fishing excursions to Mexico.

Kleinkauf is a regular at outdoor shows, stores, and clubs, where she gives slide show presentations and casting clinics, as well as demonstrations of her considerable fly tying skills.

She is a contributing editor for *Fish Alaska Magazine* and a regular contributor to many other fly fishing publications. She has been "special explorer" for the *Alaska* Magazine Television series on PBS since its inception. Her Women's Flyfishing® web site at http://www.womensflyfishing.net is the Internet's leading resource for fly fishing women.

Kleinkauf also is a member of the Worldwide

Outfitter & Guides Association, Alaska Fly Fishers, Trout Unlimited, The Federation of Fly Fishers, and The Northwest Women Flyfishers. She serves a director of the International Women Fly Fishers and a member of the professional staffs of Ross Reels, Mustad®, Hooks, and Patagonia®.

A long-time Alaskan, Michael DeYoung is well known for his stunning outdoor images. His photos have appeared in numerous magazines including *Alaska, Adventure West, National Geographic,* and *New Age Journal.* He is a regular contributor to the annual *Alaska Milepost.*

A trained meteorologist, DeYoung understands weather and light, background which enhances his photography. An avid fly fisher himself, he lives for the day when he can figure out how to cast a fly rod with one hand while simultaneously taking pictures with the other.